Hawick
in the 20th Century

Hawick

in the 20th Century

Published by Hawick Callants Club

Edited by David R H Nuttall

www.hawickcallantsclub.co.uk

Copyright © 2004 Hawick Callants Club

ISBN No. 0–9548562–0–1

Designed and printed by Buccleuch Printers Ltd., Carnarvon Street, Hawick

FOREWORD

HAWICK CALLANTS CLUB was founded in 1904 and to mark the Centenary in 2004 the Club commissioned six exhibitions to run consecutively during the year illustrating life in Hawick during the century.

These exhibitions were:
> Hawick Callants Club and Stobs Camp
> Art and Literature
> Common-Riding and Cornets
> Hawick at War
> Sporting Heroes
> Hawick Industry

During the development of the exhibitions the Club decided to make a permanent record of the information gathered and this book is the result.

The book is not intended to be a definitive history of Hawick in the 20th century but it is hoped that it will give a flavour of life during this time and will encourage the exploration of the wealth of information still available.

ACKNOWLEDGEMENTS

HAWICK CALLANTS CLUB thanks all those many individuals, companies, clubs and associations without whose generous help neither this publication nor the exhibitions held throughout 2004 would have been possible.

Special thanks to:
The staff of Hawick Museum and Drumlanrigs Tower.
Photographers Val Watts, Lesley Fraser, Derek Lunn, John Parris and Jim Rowan for the generous use of images reproduced.

Contents

Hawick Callants Club

FOUNDED 1904

THE CALLANT

His heart is warm, his hand is free,
    His love's an inspiration
For Border hill, and dale, and Hawick
    His centre of creation;
And fair or tryst aye proves the best
    To him wi' a bit brawl in't,
He'll fight the field though heids are peei'd
    He wunna yield, the Callant!

Mathew Gotterson

PRIVATE

HAWICK, 30th Nov. 1903

Dear Sir,

A MEETING to formally inaugurate a
HAWICK "CALLANTS" Club will be held in
the TOWER HOTEL, on the evening of TUESDAY
8th December at eight o'clock, which you
are respectfully invited to attend.

In view of the probable large influx
of population in the near future the time
is thought to be opportune to form this
Club, the objects of which are fully explained
on the Draft Copy of Rules, annexed.

As the Membership of the Club will be
strictly limited, we shall be glad, in the
event of you being unable to attend the
meeting, if you will communicate at once
with the Interim Secretary, Mr James Edgar,
5, High Street, as to whether you desire to
become a Member or not.

Yours faithfully,

MARTIN DECHAN	T. D. DARLING
THOMAS KER	WALTER SCOTT
ADAM LAING	WM. N. GRAHAM
A. H. DRUMMOND	HUGH ANDERSON
J. E. D. MURRAY	JAMES EDGAR

The Hawick "Callants'" Club.

T ime in its flight doth varied changes bring,
H owe'er so slow they come,
E 'en though on rapid or unhasting wing,
    Yet they come.

H and in hand we face each coming year,
A nd watch the changes, as they hurry on,
W ith close intent, lest landmarks disappear
I nto the vortex of oblivion ;
C arefully scanning custom's beaten way,
K eeping close watch on tendencies to stray.

C ustoms and rites and ceremonies grown
A ncient and hoary, all their glamour cast
L engthways along the centuries now flown,
L inking the present with the golden past ;
A nd while they tinge the old heroic days
N ow grown so distant with a rare romance,
T he charm bewitching of their quaint old ways
S eems but to strengthen as the years advance.

C arefully handed down from long ago,
L et us as carefully cherish them—our crown
U nstained, untarnished, unimpaired, and so
B anning all change until *we* also
    Hand them down.

THE KAY.

HAK 7368

The Hawick "Callants'" Club.

FIRST ——

Annual Dinner.

TOWER HOTEL,
FRIDAY, 19th Feby., 1904.

Chairman: Councillor Ker, President.
Croupier: Ex-Bailie Dechan, Vice-President.

Menu.

Soup.
VERMICELLI.   KIDNEY.

Fish.
BOILED COD.,   OYSTER SAUCE.
FRIED FILLET OF HADDOCK.   ANCHOVY SAUCE.

Joints.
ROAST SIRLOIN OF BEEF.   ROAST MUTTON
STEAK AND KIDNEY PIE.

Sweets.
SULTANA PUDDING,   APPLE TART.
MARASCHINO JELLY.
CREAMS.
COMPOTE OF FRUIT.

CHEESE.

Toast List.

"The King and Queen," - - The PRESIDENT.
"Prince and Princess of Wales, and other Members of
    the Royal Family," - - The PRESIDENT.
"The Imperial Forces," - - The PRESIDENT.
    Reply - - - Major HADDON.
"The Hawick 'Callants' Club," - The PRESIDENT.
"Our Cornets," - - Mr WALTER HUME.
    Replies   Cornet SCOTT and Ex-Cornet DRUMMOND.
"Callants in Exile" *(Rhyme and Reason)*, Mr J. E. D. MURRAY.
"Oor Ain Auld Toon," - Mr THOMAS CALDWELL.
    Reply - - - Provost MELROSE.
"Local Art and Literature," - Mr A. LAING.
    Reply - - - Mr J. G. WINNING.
"Our Local Representatives," - The VICE-PRESIDENT.
    Reply - - - Bailie SCOTT.
"Local Sports and Pastimes," - Mr W. T. GRIEVE.
    Reply - - - Mr JAMES BARRIE.
"President and Vice-President," -
    Replies - - PRESIDENT and VICE-PRESIDENT.

Founding of
Hawick Callants Club

WHEN THE WAR OFFICE bought Stobs at the beginning of the 20th Century there was much concern that the camp would be considerably enlarged and thereby a great influx of military personnel living in and around Hawick might impair what made Hawick so enjoyable for its own people and might cause the old established customs and traditions to be diluted or even lost.

These concerns prompted ten prominent townsmen to issue a letter dated 30th November 1903 to about a hundred other townsmen inviting them to attend a meeting to form "Hawick Callants Club" and attached a copy of the first draft rules.

The first formal meeting was held on 8th December 1903 and Hawick Callants Club was born with around thirty members.

The objects of the Club were, and still are:

The cultivation of local sentiment

The preservation of the ancient customs and institutions of the town of Hawick and of its history and traditions

The fostering of local art and literature

The commemoration of important local incidents

The perpetuation of the memories of worthy townsmen

Members of the Club must be connected with the town or its immediate neighbourhood by birth or descent from a native, or long residence or association, and must be supporters of the Common-Riding.

The Club comprises two hundred Ordinary members and a number of Honorary Members, Honorary Life Members and Overseas Members.

ROLL OF ORIGINAL MEMBERS

Aimers, Councillor, Wm. Cross Wynd.
Anderson, Councillor Stephen, 21 Slitrig Crescent.
Anderson, Hugh, Hazeldean Cottage.
Anderson, Robert, Bamford Woollen Mills, Rochdale.
Anderson, William, Allars Bank.

Bannerman, Dr. Geo. G. 27 Bridge Street.
Barrie, Dr. Wm. T., 18 Bridge Street.
Barrie, Ex. Provost W.S. Ashwood Wilton Hill.
Barrie, James, Rosewood.

Cairns, James, 9 Glebe View.
Caldwell, Thos. 17 Royal Park Terrace, Edinburgh.
Craw, Wm. 2 Atkinson St, Urmston Manchester.

Dechan, Ex. Bailie Martin, 29 Bridge Street.
Deachan, Francis, 29 Bridge Street.
Darling, R.D. Langsyde.
Dickson, R.H. 8 Myreslawgreen.
Drummond, A.H. 3 Buccleuch Place.
Drummond, D.O. 99 Lothian Road, Edinburgh.

Elliot, James, Flex.
Edgar, James, 14 Bridge Street.

Ferguson, James, Stanley House, Chestnut Avenue, Headingley, Leeds.

Graham, Wm. 14 Howegate.
Graham, Wm. N. 14 Howegate.
Grieve, W.T. 20 Buccleuch Terrace.

Haddon, Andrew, 1 West Stewart Place.
Haddon, Walter, Colislinn.
Henderson, Councillor J.A. 5 Loan.
Hume, Walter, Beaconsfield Terrace.

Innes, W.A. The Elms.

Jardine, Alex. 41 High Street.

Kennedy, W.P. Sandbed.
Kennedy, W. Crown Hotel.
Ker, Councillor Tom, Lockhart Place.
Kerr, A.W. 72 High Street.

Laing, Adam, 9 Buccleuch Street.
Lawson, Bailie A.S. Sandbed.

MacNee, George CH. of S. Training College, Edinburgh.
Marshall James, Linden Bank.
Melrose, Provost John, Hopehill.
Miller, Ex-Bailie John, 7 Teviot Crescent.
Milligan, Councillor Robert, Rosevale Cottage.
Mitchell, Ex-Provost Robert, Broomie Knowe.
Murray, J.E.D. 43 Bridge Street.

Oliver, Andrew R. Thornwood.
Oliver, Douglas, Thornwood.
Oliver, Wm. Eskdaill Terrace.

Paisley, James, 43 High Street.

Robertson, Peter, Grocer & Wine Merchant, Duns.

Scoon, Robert, Eskdaill Bank.
Scott, Bailie Francis, 26 High Street.
Scott, Ex-Councillor Andrew, 25 Howegate.
Scott, David, 389 Chester Road, Manchester.
Scott, Peter, Beechwood.
Scott, Tom.
Scott, W.P. Fairview.
Scott, Walter, Pilmuir.
Sheil, James, Walkerburn.
Smith, John, 16 Beaver Street, Old Trafford, Manchester.
Stoddart, Wm. 18 Bourtree Place.
Sutherland, Alex. Imperial Hotel.
Sutherland, James, Imperial Hotel.

Thompson, R.R. 10 Howegate.
Turnbull, Adam, Orrock Place.
Turnbull, John, 51 High Street.
Turnbull, Robert, 8 Buccleuch Street.
Turnbull, Wm. Tower Knowe.
Turner, J.S. Torwood.

Vernon, J.J. 81 High Street.

Wilson, Councillor G.H. Springbank.
Winning, J.G. Branxholme Knowe.

Young, Wm. Oakwood.

The Centenary Service of Dedication

18TH JANUARY 2004

Conducted and written by Rev E P Lindsay Thomson M.A. with
assistance from
Ian M Landles, Ronald W Laidlaw, David R H Nuttall

Photo: Val Watts

Hawick Callants Club

Centenary

Service of Dedication

at

Trinity Church, Hawick

on

Sunday 18th January 2004

at 2.00pm

Conducted by Rev E P Lindsay Thomson MA
Honorary Chaplain

Order of Service

Hawick Saxhorn Band will play as congregation arrives

Voluntary by Mr Archie Sanderson FTCL, Organist

Welcome

Hymn
"O Worship the King"

Prayer by Rev. Lisa-Jane Rankin

Hymn
"Be thou my vision"

Introduction
Song "The Callant" by Robert Armstrong MBE

Dedication of articles representing Club's involvement in all aspects of the town:

Hawick Callants Club
Dedicated by John Aitkin MBE
Reading and prayer by Club President Thomas M Hartop
Anthem written by Ian W Seeley, sung by Trinity Church Choir

Oor Ain Auld Toon
Dedicated by Honorary Provost Zandra Elliot
Reading and prayer by Club Vice-president Ex-Cornet Charles W McCrerie
Song "Old Mill Town" written and played by David Finnie,
sung by Deborah Lyons

Common Riding and Traditions
Dedicated by Cornet Greg McLeod
Reading and prayer by Ex-Cornet W Bruce Mactaggart (Cornet 1954)
Hymn "Invocation" by Trinity Church Choir

Education
Dedicated by Mrs Alison Robson
Reading and prayer by Club Hon Treasurer R Scott Elliot
Song "It's a New Song Beginning" by Trinity School Choir

Art, Literature and Music
Dedicated by Ian W Landles
Reading and prayer by David R H Nuttall
Hymn   "I to the Hills"

Our Borderland
Dedicated by Walter T Scott
Reading and prayer by Club Hon Secretary Ronald W Laidlaw
Song "My Borderland" by Michael C Aitken

Collection
Music by Organist

Prayer by Father Jeremy Bath

Hymn
"Rejoice the Lord is King"

Benediction

*After the service the Hawick Saxhorn Band will play the congregation
to the 1514 memorial and play there for a few minutes.*

Plaque unveiled after address by Club President Thomas M Hartop

13

Hawick Callants Club

Photo: Val Watts

"Hawick shall triumph 'mid destruction"
Was a druid's dark prediction
Strange the issues that unrolled it
Centuries after he'd foretold it.

It's not surprising therefore that the cry TO DEFEND should reach out from the soul of our town.

Aye defend your rights and common.

The cry goes up each time the song is sung and amid the relaxed, happy atmosphere of celebration of every Common Riding there is a note of resolution, **AYE DEFEND**. That note also lay behind the founding of Hawick Callants Club in 1904.

From time immemorial it had found expression in the ancient custom of riding the meiths and marches . . . a beacon of warning to greedy raiders and marauders.

It took on new meaning in the grim silence of Flodden flashing red from the swords and spears of veteran heroes. It coursed through the veins of Hawick's young callants as they left a defenceless town and made their indignant dash to Hornshole, there to defeat the enemy and capture their flag.

AYE DEFEND YOUR RIGHTS AND COMMON. After the granting of the charter in 1537 it became the glad but obligatory response of a grateful people to its generous donor . . . then in 1777 it became the adrenalin of a desperate legal battle by the Magistrates against Buccleuch.

Ten years after the founding of the Club the same cry sent Hawick Callants from our shore in defense of our nation and its hard-won liberties. The Club remembers those who fell in this war, in the next war and in lesser conflicts down to the present by laying a wreath at the War Memorial. The 60 Hawick callants who fell at Gallipoli are remembered in a wreath-laying ceremony at the 1514 Memorial.

It was a military threat of an entirely different order which prompted the founding of the Callants Club in 1904. When the War Office bought Stobs at the beginning of the 20th Century there was much disquiet in the town that the camp would be considerably enlarged. A great influx of military personnel living in and around Hawick might impair what made Hawick so enjoyable for its own people and might cause the old established customs and traditions to be diluted or even lost.

To meet this threat the Hawick Callants Club was born.

The objects of the Club were and still are:
The cultivation of local sentiment
The preservation of the ancient customs and institutions of the town of
    Hawick and of its history and traditions
The fostering of local art and literature
The commemoration of important local incidents
The perpetuation of the memories of worthy townsmen.

READING AND PRAYER
Read by President Thomas M. Hartop
Great is the Lord and most worthy of praise in the city of our God. It is
    beautiful in its loftiness, the joy of the whole earth.
God is in her citadels; He has shown himself to be her fortress.

When kings joined forces, when they advanced together,
They saw her and were astounded. They fled in terror.
As we have heard, so have we seen; in the city of the Lord Almighty, in
the city of God. God makes her secure for ever.

Amen.

Let us pray.

Lord God, you have given us a land like a promised land, and a people like a chosen people. The land is sweet to our eyes and its people touched with the milk of human kindness. Help us to defend our inheritance and live worthy of those who have bequeathed to us its freedom, its character and its traditions. We ask this prayer through Jesus Christ our Lord.

Amen.

DEDICATION – PAST PRESIDENT JOHN AITKIN MBE

I LAY HERE THIS BADGE OF OFFICE AS A TOKEN OF THE CLUB'S DEDICATION AND CONTINUING COMMITMENT TO THE FURTHERING OF ITS OBJECTIVES.

"Song "The Callant." By Mr. Robert Armstrong MBE

Oor Ain Auld Toon

DEDICATION - READ BY HON. PROVOST ZANDRA ELLIOT

Magistrates! Be faithful trustees,
Equal poise the scales of justice,
See our common rightly guidit,
Quirky lairds nae mair divide it.

The Hawick Callants Club exists not for itself but for the sake of Hawick. This perception has been held by a long line of Provosts, Honorary Provosts and Councils throughout our history. All have accepted the solemn responsibility of guarding its traditions and its Common.

Hawick has known great development, great progress and great changes down through the years but she should not lose what is unique if she is to remain in our affections as **OOR AIN AULD TOON . . . OOR BORDER HAME.**

The Callants Club's first contribution to the Town was the erection of the Ca' Knowe Memorial Cairn which was unveiled by J. G. Winning, the Club President, attended by Provost Melrose and Cornet Will Thorburn.

The Cairn is a dynamic symbol of our history.

Notice was given to the Burgesses of the Burgh and Town of Hawick that they were to ride the marches of the commonty and attend the Bailies and Council in their best apparel. The Cairn marks the spot where the Burgess Roll was called, with punishments later handed out to those who had dared to absent themselves without good cause.

The unveiling of the Cairn was just a start to the Club's determination to mark significant moments in the Town's history with memorials and plaques, and to commemorate characters who have enhanced it significantly.

Many markers now exist to perpetuate what might otherwise have been lost in the mists of time. Plaques mark the sites of The Mercat Cross, The Cobble Entry, The Auld Brig, The Four Ports, The Four Tolls, the High Street House of Bailie John Hardie who in 1771 brought the first stocking frames to Hawick, the High School in memory of Rev. Alexander Orrock whose bequest led to the founding of the Hawick Grammar School, Drumlanrig's Tower to mark the visit of Sir Walter Scott and the Wordsworths.

The Club has also cooperated with the Council and others bodies, playing a major roll in the maintenance of important monuments such as The Moat, The Henry Scott Riddell Monument, The 1514 Memorial and Hornshole . . . to mention but a few.

Generosity to public office has always been an attribute of Hawick Callants Club. As early as 1906 it organised a public subscription to purchase the first magnificent gold chain and robe of office for the Provost. More recently in 1979 the Club President presented the Honorary Provost with a new chain following the loss of the original. There has been great cooperation on many other matters.

In 1976, proposals for future Common Riding Ceremonial and Administrative Committees prepared by the Club were approved and adopted at a public meeting creating the Honorary Provost's Council, bringing a satisfactory conclusion to the work of the Council and other public bodies in this important matter.

Many Provosts and Honorary Provosts have been grateful for the Club's help and support – and for the welcome they have received at receptions and dinners.

READING AND PRAYER

Read By Vice President Ex-Cornet Charles W. McCrerie

Pray for the peace of Jerusalem. May those who love you be secure. May there be peace within your walls and security within your citadels.

For the sake of my relatives and friends I will say, "Peace be within you." For the sake of the house of the Lord our God I will seek your prosperity. How can we sing the songs of the Lord in a foreign land?

If I forget you, O Jerusalem may my right hand forget its skill.

May my tongue cling to the roof of my mouth if I do not remember you, if I do not consider you my highest joy.

Let us pray.

We ask Thee Lord, to bless oor ain auld toon, the place we love the best. May there be a reign of peace within our walls . . . of our public buildings, our factories and mills, our schools and colleges, our hospitals and old folks homes, our churches and our chapels. May there be peace in our own homes and may it reign in our community and its institutions. May there be friendship in the life of our town and fraternity in our mutual dealings. May there be prosperity for our industries and success in our commerce and in love in every heart to prosper your will among your people.

We ask this prayer in Jesus' Name

Amen.

DEDICATION – BY HON. PROVOST ZANDRA ELLIOT

I LAY HERE THIS PROVOST'S CHAIN AS A TOKEN OF THE CLUB'S CONTINUING COMMITMENT TO COOPERATE AND WORK FOR THE GOOD OF OOR AIN AULD TOON.

Song "Old Mill Town" Written & Played by David Finnie, Sung by Deborah Lyons.

Common Riding and Traditions

DEDICATION - READ BY CORNET GREG McLEOD

*Thus we boast a Muir and Colour
Won by deeds of hardy valour -
Won in fields where victory swithered
Won when Scotia's laurels withered.*

*Annual since our flag's been carried
Round our Muir by men unmarried,
Emblem grand of those who won it
Matrimonial hands would stain it.*

If the Callants Club exists for Hawick it most specifically exists for the Common Riding, the expression of our history, the gathering point of all our unique traditions. The first requirement of every member of the Callants

Club is that he should be a supporter of the Common Riding. It has been described by famous historical writer, Nigel Tranter, as the most outstanding manifestation of local spirit, tradition and patriotism to be seen in these islands or anywhere else. It pays tribute to the freedom, liberties and deliverances bought at great cost of blood and courage by our forefathers, commemorating the famous battles, raids and rides of the old days when the border was the border indeed. There is no animosity toward England ... only a fine and healthy appreciation of privileges hard-earned and a lively sense of rivalry, colour, verve and tradition. After speaking of the ride-outs which test the horsemanship and staying power of all concerned. He then goes on todescribe the real fun -its early morning breakfasts and speeches, processions, song-singing, its ceremonies, races, pageantry and junketings with curds and cream and something stronger. There is much hilarity but a certain basic solemnity too for though a vigorous and taxing business it is all done within an essential purpose and discipline within a carefully maintained time schedule.

The whole town takes part. That is the most significant aspect of it all.These are no shows, spectacles laid on for the populace to stare at and applaud by benevolent municipalities. This is the authentic expression of the peoples' emotion. Everyone joins in, from councillors down to young boys and girls let out of school for the occasion. Indeed the young callants probably provide the most gratifying and encouraging picture of all for they represent so vitally and naturally a living tradition. They struggle for the opportunity to hold the horses and lead them up and down. They dream of mounting, of hiring, of owning, of riding, of bringing back the badge that proclaims the most gruelling of the ride-out well and truly ridden. Local patriotism, love of town and countryside, its history and tradition; the corporate spirit, the long memory of moss-trooping and reiving forebears; healthy rivalry; worthy ambition to be foremost in the fray.

What other municipality in these islands would not give its mace, its chain-of-office and half its charters to see such a spirit in its townsfolk.

There you have it. An authentic history, an authentic tradition, an authentic Common Riding which comes round each year and in the Callants Club surely an authentic friend which over a hundred years has supported it, marked down its history, exemplified its fraternity and encouraged, greeted

Feted and honoured every cornet chosen to carry the flag on behalf of the town and all its stands for. Long may that be so.

READING AND PRAYER

Read by Ex-Cornet Bruce Mactaggart

Walk about Zion. Go round her, count her towers.

Consider well her ramparts. View her citadels that you amy tell of them to the next generation.

For this God is our God for ever and ever.

He will be our guide, even to the end.

Beloved, let us love one another. For love is from God.

Everyone who loves has been born of God and knows God.

Whoever does not love does not know God. For God is love.

This is how God showed his love among us. He sent his one and only Son into the world that we might live through him.

No-one has ever seen God but if we love one another God lives in us and his love is made complete in us.

Let us pray.

Grant almighty God that the flame of your Holy Spirit may burn brightly for the soul of our town. We bring our great gifts to your House and to your presence. Accept the dedication of what is dear.

Spread a spirit of love among all the people of our town, among us and among the members of this club and grant that all we do may be acceptable in your sight until in the sacrifice and mercy of your Son we reach the boundary of your eternal Kingdom.

We ask this prayer through Jesus Christ, our Lord.

Amen.

DEDICATION BY CORNET GREG MCLEOD

I LAY HERE THIS SASH IN TOKEN OF THE CLUB'S CONTINUING COMMITMENT AND DEDICATION TO THE HAWICK COMMON RIDING.

INNVOCATION - Trinity Parish Church Choir.

Education

Dedication - Read by Alison Robson

Scotia felt thine ire, O Odin,
On the bloody field of Flodden;
There our fathers fell with honour,
Round their King and Country's banner

To hear a whole school of primary children sing these words (with some undue emphasis perhaps placed on the word "bloody") at the Thursday morning visit of the Cornet, is to be assured that the spirit of the Common Riding is still alive and well among our youngest generation. Sporting their colourful rosettes and singing with verve and with smiling faces it is clear that they have already imbibed the local sentiment and are avid supporters of the Common Riding. Perhaps they would already qualify as applicants for membership of the Callants Club. A particularly delightful moment in the ceremony is when the Cornet presents the Clubs book token prizes to the winners of its annual essay competition. The winning pupil, if it's a girl, enjoys the bonus of a kiss from the Cornet and if it's a boy he is smothered in embarrassment with a kiss from the Cornet's lass.

The essay competition and its prizes was instituted in 1957 and has continued annually since then. To help pupils in their preparation — and the teachers supervising them —- a Learning Project on the Common Riding and its Traditions by Ron Taylor was subsidised by the Club and 200 hundred copies made available. This was updated in 1998 with a separate loose leaf page describing each part of the Common Riding. Pupils engage wholeheartedly in this exercise. Undoubtedly it increases their knowledge of the historical background and enhances their understanding of ceremony's true meaning. In 1999 the Hawick Callants Club David Ferguson Memorial trust was formed to honour a late member. The trust presents a geography prize at Hawick High School and awards the David Ferguson Memorial Shield for special achievement. At one stage there was also a schools competition for the singing of Hawick Songs.

It was fortuitous indeed that one of the Club's founding members was Walter Hume, headmaster of Trinity Primary School in the early years of the last century. He was the driving force behind the first schools essay competition instigated in 1909. The standards were high and I doubt if many here, aged 15 and over would care to tackle the tough questions set in exam conditions. But his vision has been continued in the Club and is productive of benefits greatly appreciated by staff and pupils in every school. This work unquestionably fulfils the basic objectives of the Club.

READING AND PRAYER

Read By Hon. Treasurer Scott Elliot

Do not forget my teaching but keep my commands in your heart. For they will prolong your life many years and bring you prosperity.

Let love and faithfulness never leave you. Bind them around your neck; write them on the tablet of your heart. Then you will win favour and a good name in the sight of God and other people.

Get wisdom; get understanding;

Do not forsake wisdom and she will protect you. Embrace her and she will honour you. She will set a garland of grace upon your head and present you with a crown of splendour.

The path of the righteous is like the first gleam of dawn, shining ever brighter till the full light of day appears.

Let us pray

Lord who came thyself to earth a child, bless all the children of our town and keep them in thy care.

Lord of all knowledge and wisdom, help us to increase the understanding of our children for the enrichment of their lives.

Lord, who has prepared for all your children an inheritance which can never wither, spoil or fade, bless the humble efforts that we make towards our children that they may grow into the rich inheritance prepared for them and walk in right ways to the honour of our town and the glory of Thy name.

We make this prayer through Jesus Christ, our Lord.

Amen.

DEDICATION BY ALISON ROBSON

I LAY HERE THE CALLANTS CLUB DAVID FERGUSON MEMORIAL SHIELD AS A SYMBOL OF THE CLUB'S CONTINUED COMMITMENT TO THE FURTHERING OF ITS OBJECT IN THE FIELD OF EDUCATION.

Song by Trinity Primary School Choir.

Art, Literature and Music

Dedication - Read by Ian W. Landles

Hail to the banner that proudly floats o' er us,
Hail to the brave hearts that bear it along,
Proudly we glance at the record before us
True hearted heroes so famous in song.

Up wi' the banner high
Hark to the gathering cry,
Dear to each heart is the old native strain
Children and bearded men
Join in the old refrain,
Shout Teriodin again and again.

Any aspiring poet or song-writer in our Borderland knows that he stands on the shoulders of giants with names like Scott, Hogg and Stevenson to inspire him and minds like Hume and Carlyle to daunt his brain.

You look at the story of our Borderland strewn with deeds of daring, deeds of pride, deeds of honour and, yes deeds of shame . . . of battles long ago and victories plucked from the jaws of hell. No wonder there's a tale in the Borders we say.

But in the inspiration of the hands that wrote it down what a tale it has become!

You look at the men of the Borders - no shortage of stout-hearted callants, men of steel, veteran heroes. No wonder there's a fable in the Borders we say.

Yes, but in the golden voice of those who rang out their fame what a fable it has become.

You look at loveliness of our border burns and woods and we say - No wonder there's poetry in the Borders, but in the imaginations of our ancient rhymers who saw goblins in the streams and fairies dancing in the woody shades what poetry it has become.

You look at the beauty of our border hills and vales. No wonder there's music in the Borders you say. Yes but in the voice of our minstrelsy what a song. Oh, what a song! And here above them all this grey auld toon is once more Queen o a' the Border.

No other town in the Borders, or in the length and breadth of our land or anywhere else in the wide world can boast the book of songs we cherish.

With stalwarts like Tom Ker and R S Craig there at its beginning it's not surprising that the Club decided that the promotion of Border Art and Literature should be one of its primary objects. They knew that the Borders and above all auld Hawick was itself a story, a poem, a song.

Here are just some of the Club's publications

1927 R S Craig Hawick and the Borders and James Turnbull Hawick in Bygone Days.

1931 A new edition of the Hawick Songs

1957 A new Hawick Song Book - music edition

1964 The first LP of Hawick Songs

1978 a new edition of Hawick in Song and Poetry and in time for this centenary . . . a new Hawick Song book with new Hawick songs and a CD.

J. B. Selkirk wrote
Ay, penter lad, thraw to the wund your canvas
This is holy grund.
Wi a' its highest art acheevin
The picter's deid and this is leevin.

But in oor art the picter's no been deid, most memorably in the lively, stirring canvases of Club Past-President Adam Robson and so oor picter's leevin, oor story's leevin and maybe above all oor song's still leevin for the Guitterbluid spirit, the CALLANT SPIRIT IS IN THE SONG.

It comes as a tender strain to some poor troubled soul and brings some comfort to assuage his fears, it comes unbidden "to the exile who's long been a-rovin".

It flows through the community like a tide of Teviot and gathers us as one.

It gallops like 400 horsemen in yeh streekit line soaring to the skies like the fluttering pennon that it follows. It is the living legacy of Hawick. And still it will go on for there will aye be poetry babbling in our burns and music flowing from our hills for as long as Slitrig dances doon the glen to join the Teviot Water.

READING AND PRAYER

Read by Past President David R. H. Nuttall

Psalm 121 adapted.
I will lift my eyes to the hills whence comes my help,
To the Eildon Hills, the Minto Hills, the slopes of Ruberslaw,
To the Vertish, then to Penchrise and to Pilmuir Rig and the Maiden Paps.
They are my inspiration and my help.
My safety comes from the God who made them . . . the God who made both Heaven and earth.
He alone will keep our feet from sliding. While He watches over us He will not sleep. He is awake to our needs. Against the winter sleet he'll be our shield and in the summer sun the shade at our right hand.
He will watch over us day and night.
He shall preserve our soul . . . preserve us from all ill.
With the Lord it will be safe oot, safe in
For Hawick, for all of life, for ever and for ever.

Amen.

Let us pray.
Almighty God, canvas that contains the whole picture from the beginning to the end. The music of the universe, Voice that spoke and called the world to be, Word before the human poet spoke, song of everlasting praise. We bow before Thee and Thy works. In songs of love and songs of history help us to hear an everlasting song. In momentary glimpses may we see a vision

of eternal things. Inspire us still and help us to find words to tell the inspiration of our hearts. We ask this prayer through Jesus Christ, our Lord.

Amen.

DEDICATION - BY IAN W. LANDLES

I LAY HERE THE NEW HAWICK SONG BOOK, SYMBOL OF THE CALLANTS CLUB CENTENARY, SYMBOL OF ITS CONTINUING COMMITMENT TO THE ART AND LITERATURE OF OUR BORDERLAND.

Hymn - I to the hills.

Rev. E. P. Lindsay Thomson, M.A., and Trinity Church Choir

Photo: Val Watts

Our Borderland

Dedication - Read by W. T. Scott

My Borderland, My Borderland,
The sweetest spot I know,
As all things fair and all things rare
Have proudly deem'd it so,
And by God's light that sparkles bright
In all things nobly plann'd
With joyful heart, till death us part,
I'll love my Borderland.

A whaup rises from the tussock grass holding our eye for a commanding moment as it scurries to protect its young. But it's a small phenomenon compared with the breadth of moor. That's our Borderland.

We take a well-worn track and scale a hill and find we're on the edge of a wilderness, as yet uncultivated and untouched by hand of man, that stretches out beyond. That's our Borderland . . . the vast backdrop of nature that contains the busy industry of our working and our private lives . . . the silence that still speaks to us beyond the roar of traffic and the rhythm of the mills . . . The panoramic rim of inspiration that contains our town within its arms bidding us to reach up and out to new horizons calling . . . That's our Borderland . . . beautiful, wonderful . . . in the rippling view we see from Grundison. . . . in the lovely valleys that we know so well.

But our Borderland is more than this

'Tis not the birds in springtime
Bringing music to the trees,
'Tis not the flowers of summer
Lending fragrance to the breeze
'Tis the gentle touch of kindness
From the ever helping hand
That drives all care and sadness from
My own dear Borderland.

Johnston is right. The Borderland is people as well as land. It's both character and terrain. It's both context and community . . . enriching, satisfying, fulfilling . . . It is our Eden BUT IT'S MORE

It's our STORY and our history and our folklore all in one. It's where the past still marches up on us and meets us where we are. It's where battles fought so long ago are still being fought within the ceremonies of our imagination and our thoughts. It's where families and the generations of them still mean something. It's our sense of honour . . . Our identity. BUT IT'S MORE.

No one can ever say precisely what it our Borderland for it's like another world. Despite the Border even maps will not describe it. And Councils when they draw their boundaries define but the parameters of their sway.

But if you're in some far off place and returning here again you know you're in the Borderland when you feel as sense of HAME.

So come and A wull show ti ee
The spot that means the world ti me,
The place ma hert aye longs ti be'
Auld Hawick ma Border hame.

Ian speaks for all of us. Surely there's no one here who hasn't such a place!

Is it where Slitrig dances doon the glen. Or where the Teviot slowly glides.

Is it somewhere on the Mair or on the Miller's Knowes. Is it in some quiet place with peace and trees and flowers. Is it where a loved one lies or where a pledge of love was given. Somewhere in our Borderland there's a place where to commune with nature is to commune with God . . . to drink the wonder is to see the hand of God. It's a place where love is a confession and the thought of love won't go away. It's our Borderland and a place that's truly Hame.

No wonder that our forebears fought for it and gave their blood to hold it and to hand it to their bairns. And it's ours, and we'll protect it and we'll honour it and we'll love it and we'll treasure it. It's our heritage. It's our everything and as such we'll hand it on.

READING AND PRAYER

Read by Club Hon. Secretary Past President Ronald W. Laidlaw

Lord, you have assigned to me, my portion and my cup;
You have made my lot secure.
The boundary lines have fallen for me in pleasant places;
Surely I have a delightful inheritance.

I will praise the Lord who counsels me.
Even at night my heart instructs me.
I have set the Lord always before me.
Because He is at my right hand I will not be shaken.

Therefore my heart is glad and my tongue rejoices
My body also will rest secure because you will not abandon me to the grave. Nor will you let your chosen one to see decay.
You have made known to me the path of life;
You will fill me with joy in your presence, with eternal pleasures at you right hand.

Let us pray
Lord, thou hast been our dwelling place in all generations.
Before the hills in order stood, or earth received her frame,
From everlasting thou art God, to endless years the same
Under the shadow of thy throne, thy saints have dwelt secure,
Sufficient is thine arm alone and our defence is sure.

So we commit our Borderland to you. Help us to guard it, to nurture it and to tend it. Help us to enrich its life . . . Protect the honour of its name

And when we hand it on may it be beautiful and lovely as we received from your hand. So help us Lord, in Jesus' Name

Amen.

Dedication By W. T. Scott

HERE I LAY THIS SOD. CUT FROM THE CA KNOWE, CUT FROM THE COMMON...A FRAGMENT OF OUR BORDERLAND ... SYMBOL OF THE CLUB'S COMMITMENT TO OUR HERITAGE OOR BORDERLAND.

Song "My Borderland" Sung by Michael C. Aitken.

COMMEMORATIVE PLAQUE UNVEILED AT 1514 MEMORIAL

President Thomas M. Hartop unveils the Plaque.

Stobs Camp, Hawick

Compiled by
Jake L. Coltman

The military camp

IN OCTOBER 1902, the government purchased Stobs Estate for use as a military camp and over a period of almost 60 years there were many changes to the 4000 acre site, which had been the ancient Borders home and lands of the Elliots of Stobs Castle.

The military moved in early 1903 adapting the area for the training of troops, rifle range and manoeuvres for cavalry and infantry regiments. Within a few months up to 20,000 troops were under canvas – hence it was dubbed "Scotland's Aldershot". Officers were accommodated in Stobs Castle and by 1907 the first of several huts were erected for the troops. Initially it was used as a summer only camp.

During the First World War it became a prisoner of war camp. At the start of the 1914–18 conflict, 575 POW camps were opened in Britain, about 24 of those were in Scotland. Many were purpose built, but others, such as Stobs, were not. To accommodate the prisoners, huts were erected providing for 6000 POW's. The first to arrive were German and Austrian civilians who arrived on a special train from Edinburgh in November 1914. Three categories of prisoners were held during the course of the war: civilian, "enemy aliens" who had settled in Britain before 1914 and now were perceived as spies; civilian passengers and seamen taken from merchant vessels and passenger liners; and military prisoners captured on the battlefield or high seas.

They were employed carrying out building work and maintenance in the camp and as work parties on surrounding farms. They received food parcels from relatives in Germany, staged plays and concerts and even had their own newspaper, "Stobsiade", which was set up at the camp and printed at Scott and Paterson, prior to being sent back to their loved ones back home in the "Fatherland". At the end of the "war to end wars", Stobs reverted to a training camp for the next 40 years.

During the Second World War only a small number of German POW's, 30 to 40, were kept at Stobs. They were work parties from a camp at Longniddry in East Lothian. At the conclusion of the 1939–45 war, Stobs became a re-settlement camp for 2000 members of the Polish Armed Forces, prior to repatriation, but a few remained in Hawick and married local girls.

There were reports in 1947 that the camp was to be extended to cover 22,000 acres but nothing materialised. During the early 1950s, volunteer units, the local K.O.S.B. regiment and men on National Service used the once again "summer only" complex.

The Ministry of Defence began phasing out many of the country's training camps and Stobs became one of them. The huts and equipment were sold, dealers coming from all over the country and by June 1959 the dismantling of Stobs was complete and the land sold for grazing.

Little remains today of what was at one time a vast military compound. The 42 prisoners who died there during the First World War and were buried in the graveyard among the trees at the camp were disinterred in 1962 and reburied in the military cemetery in Staffordshire. Only one of the wooden huts used by the POW's remains standing, as are a few brick buildings and, as each year passes, the tarmac road surfaces become more and more overgrown. Soon even the layout of the camp will be unrecognisable, leaving only the picture postcards of yesteryear to tell its story and show what it was like in its heyday and what a valuable contribution it made to the training of Britain's fighting forces.

Jake Coltman.

Prisoners arriving at Stobs station, 1915.

Getting the rolls at 6 in the morning, July 1910.

Royal Engineers digging fortifications at the camp, August 1906.

Time to relax for the Black Watch, 1903.

Preparing for kit inspection, July 1904.

46

Royal Scots among the first troops to

Cavalry Camp at Stobs.

RH

Soton

Cavalry regiment horses, July 1904.

Galloway Rifles arriving at Stobs station, July 1905.

Camp kitchen.

Soldiers of the K.O.S.B. pictured at Stobs.

Gordon Highlanders leaving the railway station on their way to Stobs, April 1915.

A spartan morning wash in the Barns Burn.

The camp at the start of the Second World War.

Group of German prisoners.

Troop train leaving Stobs station.

Prisoner of war compound.

A selection of German POW correspondence

Festive season card sent by Willi Ohms to his wife, Anne, in Herford, Germany in 1916.
"I know where my heart is at Christmas".

Mail from Kurt Stenper, Hut 151, a civilian internee, December 1915. Under the Geneva
Convention prisoners were allowed letters to their home and relatives sent free, postage 1d
to be paid on others. Shows Stobs Camp censor mark.

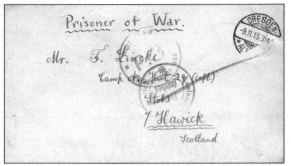

Letter sent from a boy in Dresden to his father, F. Lincke, Hut 29, a P.O.W. at Stobs, November 1915. Shows British and German censor marks.

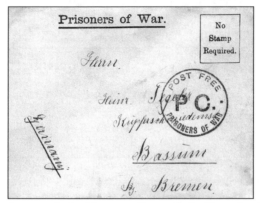

Sent by Johann Sandmann, who had been a sailor on the battle cruiser S.M.S. Blücher, the pride of the German fleet, sunk at the Battle of Dogger Bank, January 1915. Shows British censor mark.

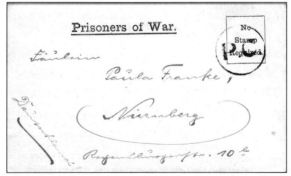

Lettersheet from Albert Schmidt, Hut 120, to Nuremberg, April 1919.

Kriegsgefangenen - Lager,
STOBS, Schottland.

Weihnacht, 1915.

"Hallo Stobs!!"

Grosse Weihnachtsrevue.

mit Musik (Chor u. Orchester), Gesang und Tanz,
CORPS DE BALLET Unter Mitwirkung hervoragender
Kuenstler.

Regie : F. Hoffmeyer.

Musik komponiret und arrangiert von E. Beu.

Dramatische Scenen und Text verfasst von H. Beckmann,
E. Behrens, A. Hotes, B. Katz und O. Kriesche.

Kostueme aus dem Atelier W. Fr. Schulz.

VERANSTALTET

vom Komitee der Civil-Lager mit guetiger Erlaubnis
des Kommandanten Lieut.-Colonel Bowman.

Praesident—RUDOLF RADBRUCH.

Geschaeftsfuehrung—FR. JAEHKEL und E. ROMMEL.

Regisseur—F. HOFFMEYER.

Musikalische Leitung—E. BEU.

Scott & Paterson, Printers, Hawick.

Christmas revue programme, 1915.

54

Nr. 3 (17).　　　ERSCHEINT DREIWOCHENTLICH.　　　26. November 1916.

Stobsiade

Zeitung des deutschen Kriegsgefangenen-Lagers STOBS in Schottland

Anschrift: „NEUE STOBSER ZEITUNG", Stobs, Schottl.　　　This paper has been submitted to the Censor.

Bezug in Deutschland: halbjaehrl. — 9 Nrn. — Mk. 1.50; bei Dauerbezug von 3—8　　Geld an: Liebesgabenstelle, Erfurt, Weisstrauengasse 4, Postscheck-Konto Leipzig
Stueck je Mk. 1.10, von mehr als 8 je Mk. 1.—, wenn an einen Bezieher gesandt.　　Nr. 21881. — Bei spaeterem Eintritt Nachlieferung der erschienenen Nrn

Beherzigung.

Feiger Gedanken
Bängliches Schwanken,
Weibisches Zagen,
Aengstliches Klagen
Wendet kein Elend,
Macht dich nicht frei.

Allen Gewalten
Zum Trutz sich erhalten,
Nimmer sich beugen,
Kräftig sich zeigen,
Rufet die Arme
Der Götter herbei.

　　　　　　　　　Goethe.

DIE DRITTE NUMMER sucht in STOBS TRAEUMT und dem Gedicht SCHWEIZER FIEBER die Stimmung festzuhalten, welche die „Schweizer Tage" im Gefangenenleben auslösen. — UNSERE POST kennen zu lernen, wird gerade für die nahe Weihnachtszeit den Freunden daheim willkommen sein. — Eine zusammenfassende Darstellung finden die vielen seit Beginn des Winterhalbjahres gehaltenen VORTRAEGE in der Lagerchronik.

Stobs traeumt . . .

Das ruhige Gleichmass des Lebens in Stobs wird von Zeit zu Zeit jählings unterbrochen. Im allgemeinen hat der Stacheldrahtbürger ja gelernt, sich über das quälende Vergleichen eines Kriegsgefangenendaseins mit einem Leben in Freiheit hinwegzuhelfen; der von uns hat glücklicherweise an der einen oder anderen Stelle mit der Tat begonnen, dem einzigen Mittel, das auf die Dauer (oder wenigstens für längere Zeit) wirklich die trüben Gedanken bannt. Dazu kam uns dann noch die gütige Mutter Natur zu hilfe, die die Erinnerung mit dem Quadrate der Entfernung (wenigstens so ungefähr) vom Erlebnis abnehmen lässt. Nach diesem wohl ganz besonders für Kriegsgefangene geschaffenen Gesetze verlieren sich beim gewöhnlichen Menschen die greifbaren Begriffe für Dinge, mit denen er lange nicht in Berührung gekommen ist, langsam immer mehr und mehr. Und es ist klar: alles das, dessen Schönheit man nicht mehr empfinden kann, entbehrt man auch nicht mehr. Dieser glücklichen Einrichtung zufolge sind zum mindesten uns alten, allzualten Gefangenen Begriffe wie Federbett, Einsamkeit, Schweinebraten und viele, viele andere mehr oder weniger — meistenteils mehr — abhanden gekommen.

Bis auf die Kameraden, die gerade an einem toten Punkt angelangt sind, herrscht also in unserem Innern ziemliche Ruhe, unter anderem Verhältnissen mit Oede und Leere bezeichnet. Aber auf des Herzens tiefstem Grunde liegt er nur desto gieriger auf der Lauer, der Tiger, Lebenshunger genannt. Wehe, wenn er eine Gelegenheit erspäht, aufzuspringen und uns mit sich zu reissen in den wilden Strudel ungestillten Verlangens!

Diese Gelegenheit bietet sich ihm von Zeit zu Zeit. Da geht raunend Frau Saga durchs Lager und flüstert einem ins Ohr: nächstens erscheinen die Schweizer Aerzte. Und nicht mehr lange, so heisst's wirklich: nächste Woche sind sie da; wer sich untersuchen lassen will, ob er „schweizfähig" ist, soll sich melden, Schweiz!? Wir alle ohne Ausnahme suchen uns mit den verblassten Erinnerungen aus früheren Zeiten, da wir noch die goldene Freiheit genossen (o wie dünkt es uns so lange, lange her!), vorzustellen, was für ein Leben sich uns in der Schweiz bieten würde, welch ein Gefühl uns überkäme, wenn plötzlich alle die Schranken des Stacheldrahts abfielen.

Es ist uns zumute wie im Märchen . . . In der Ferne lockt uns Helvetia: Komm nur zu mir, in der reinen Grösse meiner Berge soll dir wohl werden . . .

Ach, wir träumen ihn alle, den Schweizer Traum. Jeder fühlt wieder seine alten Wunden schmerzen, alle Leiden, die wir jemals zu haben wähnten, tauchen wieder auf, gewinnen wieder Gestalt. Wir beobachten uns selbst, und allmählich bildet sich fast ein jeder ein, er sei wirklich nicht gesund. Beim einen ist's die Lunge, bei m andern das Herz. Aber die brennende Krankheit. die wir wirklich haben, ist bei den meisten „nur" das Sehnen: frei sein, unter zufriedenen Menschen leben, frei seine Kräfte auswirken können.

Ganz Stobs lebt in diesen Tagen in einem Taumel hoffender Vorfreude. Die übliche Begrüssung mit dem trivialen Wort „Mahlzeit" weicht der Frage: „Meldest Du Dich auch?", und auf ein „ja!" des andern entspinnt sich eine längere Aussprache über die gegenseitigen Aussichten, in die Schweiz zu kommen. Diesmal, meint jeder, müssen sie mich mitnehmen. Nur einige wenige glaub's, die hoffen nicht mehr: sie hatten sich schon das vorige Mal mit einer Anzahl rein eingebildeter oder doch in der Phantasie stark vergrösserter Leiden zur Untersuchung eingefunden und sie als gesund wieder verlassen. Die sind Skeptiker geworden. Aber den anderen hängt der Himmel voller Bassgeigen: es kann diesmal nicht schief gehen! Man beginnt ein wenig faul zu werden; was soll man die letzten Tage noch gross tun?! Mit einem Fusse steht man doch schon in den Schweizer Bergen!

Und dann kommen sie, die Langerwarteten, die Militärärzte aus der Schweiz. Wie viele haben sich gemeldet. Tage dauert es, bis man „drankommt", bis man vor ihnen steht. All die neugeborenen Leiden werden hergezählt: hilft das eine nicht, so wird's doch wohl das andere! Aber ach, bei den Meisten ein Kopfschütteln

Art and Literature

Compiled by
Ex-Cornet A. Philip Murray
David R H Nuttall

Art and Literature

Amongst the founders of the Callants Club were many who ranked with the literary giants of their time in Hawick. Many of the songs and poems written by these men became the foundation of an unrivaled collage of work portraying the beauty of our Borderland, our rich history and tradition, and the "change or twae time has wrocht on kirk and shop and mill" through the collections compiled by the Callants Club of portraits of Hawick in Song and Poetry.

It is little wonder then that much of the work of the Callants Club over the Century has been to encourage the creative abilities not only of Teries but of writers, singers and poets throughout the Borders. We cannot give here a full anthology of the work created during the Century and only seek to whet the appetite of the reader to find for themselves the legacy we are privileged to have at our finger tips.

Over the century three editions of "Hawick in Song and Poetry" and three publications of "Music of the Songs" of Hawick have been printed.

Adam Grant produced the first edition of "Hawick Songs". He wrote and revised the accompaniments for the twenty songs included and his interpretation was the standard for many years.

Adam Ingles edited a new edition and collection for the Callants Club in 1957. Adie added some new songs, some of his own composition and simplified many of Adam Grant's arrangements bringing them up to date. On first sight his new accompaniment for "Meda's Song" looks more complicated as it reflects the tinkling

of a burn as it flows through our Borderland. This was written in the style used by Willie Lightheart, a great pianist of the time, to accompany his friend John Peden and complement his wonderful tenor voice as he sang this great song.

Ian Seeley was asked by the Callants Club to update and edit the Song Book in 2000. Ian again updated and revised many of the accompaniments and added nineteen new songs, for a number of which he wrote the musical score, and

five were his own compositions.

"Hawick in Song and Poetry" books produced could on each occasion have been

Photo: D Lunn

many times their size since poets in Hawick and the Borders have been prolific. We try here to give a flavour of the poets and their work.

Will H. Ogilvie will feature in most selections of Border poets so perhaps it is fitting to let him lead us in to our Borderland with this poem "The Gateway".

THE GATEWAY.

Come through the purple gateway
    Where Cheviot reigns supreme,
With all his glens in shadow,
    And all his heights agleam;
And look on this fair country,
    Green grassed and heather belled,
That holds the hearts of lovers
    As no land yet has held.

Lean low and hear the whisper
    Of little peat fed rills
That bid the brown Jed Water
    Go winding through the hills,
And watch the clouds on Keilder
    And see the shadows reel,
Like drunken giants homewards
    Across the braes o' Peel.

Will H. Ogilvie

A fair land, never fairer
    Than when September lays
Its colour on the woodlands
    Along the well known ways
Where heather bell is fading
    And gold the bracken turn,
From Ettrick Pen to Edgerston,
    From Kale to Langhope Burn.

There may be grander mountains,
    There may be richer leas,
There may be prouder rivers
    That tumble to the seas,
But give me this brown country,
    Grey coated, dyked and stelled,
That holds the hearts of exiles
    As no land yet has held.

From this gateway the view of the Border leaves you in no doubt from whence the artists' and the poets' inspiration comes.

The beauty that surrounds the upper Teviotdale hills down to the meeting place of Teviot and Slitrig waters in 'Oor Ain Auld Toon' has inspired the creative mind for centuries. From here you can see the rolling hills and green valleys of our Border Country, now, thankfully, a place of peace as well as beauty. It takes little imagination however to recall the time of conflict, a time which shaped the still evident independent spirit of the Borders.

John Leyden gave inspiration to many when he wrote;

Boast! Hawick Boast thy structures reared in blood
    Shall rise triumphant over flame and flood
Still doomed to prosper since on Flodden's Field
    Thy sons a hardy band, unwant to yield
Fell with their Martial King, and (glorious boast}
    Gained proud renown where Scotia's fame was Lost

And **Sir Walter Scott** in his **Sweet Teviot**
    Sweet Teviot on thy silver tide
The glaring balefires blaze no more
    No longer steel clad warriors ride
Along thy wild and willowed shore.

Writers such as these prompted and inspired the creative aspirations of the Teries and Borderers of the 20th Century.

Tom Kerr or Tee Kay as he was known, was the first President of the Callants Club. His book 'Some Thoughts O' Mine in Song and Verse' is a collection of his notable poems and songs with amongst them 'The Fairest Spot O' A' and two versions of the well loved "I Like Auld Hawick The Best".

The second version is not widely known and we leave it to the reader to compare.

"I LIKE AULD HAWICK THE BEST" (SECOND VERSION)

Though the southern skies are bluer,
    With no touch of tinge or gloom,
Though the snows and frosts are fewer
    Where the orange blossoms bloom;
Though the birds have rarer plumage
    Where the myrtle groves they nest,
And the flowers have richer bloomage-
    Yet I like auld Hawick the best.

I like auld Hawick the best,
    Each hill with heathery crest
That guards the grey auld toon below-
    I like auld Hawick the best.

Though an earthquake oft alarmeth
    'Neath the radiant eastern gleam,
Where the scenic grandeur charmeth
    With the glamour of a dream,
Though the sun looks down benignly
    Where beneath the palms we rest,
And all Natures smiles divinely-
Yet I like auld Hawick the best.

I like auld Hawick the best,
    In sylvan beauty dressed,
'Mid summer's sun and winter's snow-
    I like auld Hawick the best.

Tom Kerr (Tee Kay)
Founding President, 1904.

I have seen some mountain corries
    Glistening in the morning dew,
And have revelled in their glories
    When the sunset tinged their hue.
I have roamed the isles enchanting
    Washed by waves that never rest,
Leaving memories heart-haunting-
    But I like auld Hawick the best.

I like auld Hawick the best,
    Where'er may be my quest,
From eastern gleam to western glow-
    I like auld Hawick the best.

R. S. Craig, another founder member of the Club, together with **Adam Laing** wrote "The Hawick Tradition of 1514", taken to be the "Bible" of Hawick Tradition up to 1900. Craig also wrote "A History of Hawick and The Borders" and many poems such as.

QUEEN OF THE MOORLANDS

Old town among the Border hills;
    Grey warder of the moors!
What though to-day have clashing mills,
    Your old-world Moat endures.
By nights you dream of Flodden yet
    While Teviot seeks the sea,
What though your days in toil are set,
    You have your history!

What though at times the moorland mist
    Creeps up by wynd and street,
Your spires peer out above, sun-kist,
    To guide the stumbling feet!
Your children love you. Border town,
    O'er leagues of raging sea,
Your image calls them, looking down
    Through mists of memory!

TO TEVIOT . . .

Surely with dance the fairies greet
    Your first glad leap to riverhood,
And surely could I hear their feet
    Trip tinkling, as a fairy's should,
Meet music, Teviot, for your silver stream,
    I then might write of which I now but dream

A DREAM OF FLODDEN

Was it a sigh of yesterday, or an echo of long ago?
    The dream of an idle moment, or the real thing pictured so?
I thought that I was somewhere in the heart of that elder world,
    Where stubborn men were gathered with their battle flags unfurled.

And a favourite of many

THE MOSSTROOPERS

The lonely birds are screaming,
    The autumn light is low,
The Border hills are dreaming
    Of their battles long ago.
By moor and moss and river,
    To the swish of swathed grass,
And burnside reeds aquiver,
    The dead mosstroopers pass.

The dim light shows their faces,
    So grim and white and wan,
Through well-remembered places
    They seek the foe till dawn.
Their lips are set for battle,
    Their eyes are fierce and bright,
Their horses' bridles rattle
    In the silence of the night,

The autumn winds are sighing
    And moaning where they ride,
They greet the dead and dying
    And never one beside.
Where lonely graves are scattered,
    And ruined castles stand,
The holy cross is shattered
    By the red unchristened hand.

For them no dreamless sleeping,
    The earth gives up her dead,
The secrets in her keeping
    Flit spectral overhead,
The moonbeams tip their lances,
    Their horses stir the grass,
Amid the fairy dances
    The dead mosstroopers pass.

The watching shepherds fear them,
 They dread the crash of spears,
The lonely cattle hear them
 When lost to human ears
They meet by ground unhallowed,
 They part at break of day,
Where never man has followed,
 They pass in mist away.

J. E. D. Murray, also a founder
member of the Club, tried his hand at most
creative avenues and was successful in
each. Cornet in 1890 he went on to be
Acting Father four times and is recognized
as one of the fathers of the way we
celebrate our civic traditions today. He
became one of the most respected of true
Hawick men. He wrote a poem as a 14 year
old on Hornshole Bridge simply called

J.E.D. Murray

HORNSHOLE

Thy Fathers here have fought and bled
 To keep their country free,
Though many years since then have sped-
 They shed their blood for thee!
They met the boasting English here:
 Though they were callants then,
Their hearts were bold,they knew no fear,
 But fought like full grown men!

They 'venged their fathers who had died
 On Flodden's bloody field;
Though some of them for quarter cried,
 No mercy did they yield!
After the bloody fight was done,
 In here they threw the slain;
Then took the standard they had won ,
 And marched off home again!

That was the boy. The man left us with a legacy of songs of poetry and of pictures. Poems such as "The Reekie Howe", "Lest We Forget", "The Nicht Afore The Morn", and his many songs put to music by his friend Adam Grant; "The Wail of Flodden", "Meda's Song", "Invocation", "Clinty's Song", and with music by A. N. McL. College.

THE MOSSTROOPERS SONG

A ken o' a stream lang streekit an' blue
    That brings quaint thochts as it wammuls oot thro',
It flows thrae lang syne an' wumplin alang,
    Keeps aye croonin' owre an auld Border sang,
The braes that it laps seem glintin' o' gold,
By ages oo coont the time it has roll'd.
An' year after year as June days draw nigh,
    A horseman stands guard wi flag tae the sky.

He also wrote, produced and directed plays and musicals for the amateur stage with music provided by **Adam Grant**, amongst these were such gems as "The Gutterbludes", "The Witch O'the Wisp Hill" and "A Legend of Old Mosspaul".

John Edward Dodd Murray the photographer left a record of life in the early 20th Century and his poems and songs still inspire the young Teries of today.

James Edgar is the last founder member we single out. He was the first Hon. Secretary of the Club. A printer and publisher and Editor of "The Hawick Express" and a dedicated local historian, James wrote a number of books on life in Hawick, "Hawick in the Early Sixties" (1860s) being perhaps the most well known. President of the Callants Club in 1924, he did his part in keeping literature to the fore in the Club's development.

In 1918 he printed a column in "The Hawick Express" in the form of a letter from a true Teri. "Betty Whutson's Letter" became an institution for over 60 years.

James Edgar, editor Hawick Express, original Betty Whutson.

Written in the Teri dialect it was an often biting comment on the Town affairs. No prominent members or working folk, no event or action within the town or indeed the world was safe from the down to earth gossip style of "Betty Whutson".

Over the next 60 years James Edgar was followed as the 'Ghost Writer' by Robert H.Laidlaw, John Dodds, Bert Leishman, R.E.(Dick) Scott and Ian Landles.

A letter from the17th May 1972 read:

HAIL TO THE BANNER

Dear Maister Editor,

Aw sei that the Toon Cooncil er teh replace oor Banner Blue that hes hung in Hexam Priory for abune 60 eer. Aw've heard threh seeveral quarters that the yin that's there's in an owfeh state an no a bit worthy o' the flag that oo think seh muckle o'. The tattered relic that hings in yon sacred buildin was a gift threh the Cooncil sune efter the new nave was built and dedicateet in 1908.

Mebbe the paragraph in your paper didneh convey muckle teh the general public. What for shood the Haaick Toon Cooncil get thum anither flag? Let's try and explain an clear the grund in case there's ony misunderstannin. Aw ken only ower weel, threh the quaistshions aw get askeet, that there's a deplorable lack o' knowleege aboot the flag that the Comet cairries at the Common-Ridin. That's something that everybody that ca's heisel a Teri shood ken. 1514 an aw' that!

The eer efter Flodden that sad defeat whan Scotland was under-strength and the referee was biased, a huge English airmy under Lord Dacre cam north yince again teh make suire that oor nashion was kept in the junior league so teh speak. The English king, the notorious Henry the Eeht was worried in case the Scots hed ony thochts aboot gettin back inteh the First Division! Dacre was the warden o' the English Border Middle Mairches an keepin the peace was yin o' heis worries. Now amang the sodgers hei gathered for heis foray ower the Border war a number o' the tenants o' ferms belangin teh Hexam Priory. The tenants hed teh provide a certain amount o' militery service muckle against their wull. It's kent that the kirk in Hexam hed 35 ferms in Northumberland alane bit oo dinneh ken how mony men they provideet on that occashion.

Yin can read a lot aboot this raid on the Borders threh the dispatches Dacre sent back teh the King in London. Oo lairn that heis airmy destroyed everything they cood richt up Ewes, doon Ti'etdale afore tumin up the

Borthwick, an then gaun doon the Yill Waitter. But hei never menshions the setback teh pairt o' heis forces at a place ca'd Trows that oo now ken iz Homshole. It appears that the Hexam secshion hed left the main body an war makin their way back teh the Border. Oo a' ken how they campeet for the nicht an how they got the worst o' a fecht wi' a bunch o' callants threh Haaick whae captured their flag an brocht eet in triumf inteh the toon. That's the flag oo think seh muckle o'.

It's weel enuff established that the ancient airms o' Hexam was a gold saltire cross on a blue grund, yet somewhere ower the eers reed strips appeared on the Haaick flag. This caused a lot o' local argei-in so in 1903 the Toon Cooncil wrote teh the Lyon Court o' Airms, the heraldry folk, askin their opeenion. The answer cam back that the true colours war the colours o' Hexam. Blue an gold - so the intrusive reed was taen oot for guid.

In 1908 Provost Melrose was a guest at Hexam at the consecrashion o' the new nave, alang wi' the Burgh Officer, John Waldie. In the processhion throwe the toon, the Haaick flag, on loan be request, was cairriet an exciteet a lot o' interest. Sune efter oor ane cooncil presented the Hexam authorities wi' a replica teh hing in the nave. So nae wunder it's fa' in teh bits efter a' they eers.

Aw sei that Hexam hev gladly accepteet anither flag an that the handin ower hes teh be an offishial occashion. That's a nice jesture on their pairt an they hev inviteet Haaick tae take pairt in some big celebrashions in 1974 teh mark the 1300 anniversary o' the Priory's foondashion. It shows that the Hexam folk henneh forgotten their auld flag, or how Haaick's lookin efter 't for thum.

What reely happened at Homshole in 1514 naebody kens. Dacre dusneh menshion the defeat teh the crabbit King Henry else hei micht hev hed teh anser for't. Nor div oo ken what was the fate o' the Northumbrian tenants whae lost their flag. Thaim that survived the fecht war mabbe feered teh gan hyimm athoot eet an wullinly bade in Haaick, espaishially whan they saw oor bonny lasses!

Betty Whutson

N.B. The Flag carried by our Cornet Drew Martin in 1971 was presented to Hexham Priory in October 1972.

69

William Landles whose weekly newspaper column 'Thought For the Week' under the pseudonym "Quartus" was another long running series based on William's strongly held Christian beliefs which made us look at our life and times and our part in it. He also made us the richer by his many songs and poems among them Borthwick Water, Hame Toon and perhaps the most well known

William Landles

THE EXILE'S RETURN

Ye're welcome, sakes ye're welcome
  Where ye're gled nae doobt to be;
The wanderlust has held ye lang
  Across the wide saut sea;
The fremmit freends ye neebor there
  Are neebor-like and grand,
But ye're back now wi' your ain folk
  And we're gleg to grip your hand.

Books of his poems were published, "A Breath Frae the Hills", "Gooseberry Fair", "Penny Numbers" and "The Turn of the Year", together with compilations of his "Quartus" articles under the titles "I to the Hills", "All Good Gifts Around Us" and "Roving Commission". All are worth the read and indeed a revisit.

Ian W Landles, son of William, is also leaving his footsteps on the path of Hawick literature. During the later part of the 20th Century he has taken centre stage not only with his songs and poems but also as a speaker and performer.

Ian, principal teacher of history at Hawick High School, has taken the mantle of local historian and records the changing life of the town for posterity. His winter night classes at the High School on Hawick and its history have grown in

Ian W. Landles
Photo: Jim Rowan

popularity over the years - a 'must do' for every Teri. Ian's writing is often full of humour and it conveys his love for his home town and her inhabitants, as well as reflects the life of by-gone days. A typical sample is

THE VERTISH HILL
by Ian W. Landles

> Some folk ir juist born fortunate
>> And A am yin o thaim
> For fate decreed that Hawick
>> Among the hills should be ma hame
> A've aye been awfih gratefih
>> And a' ma life A will
> That A bide here in the toon
>> That lies ablow the Vertish Hill

MY TEVIOT VALLEY
by Ian W. Landles

> Often I dreamt of my dear Teviot Valley,
> Home that I left all those long years ago,
> Then I was young and I had all the answers,
> There was very little that I didn't know.
> The wide world it beckoned, the fer gress seemed greener,
> The bright lights they lured me like a moth to a flame.
> I wandered the earth and I sailed its great oceans,
> In search of fulfilment, of fortune and fame.
>
> Now I've returned to my own Teviot Valley,
> My exile is over, my spirit is free.
> Here hearts I love beat, I'm back wi ma ain folk,
> Home once again where I've long wished to be.
> The summer sun shines as I sit in the silence
> Looking doon on ma hame frae the target hill's crest
> Weel-kent are the streets and familiar the places
> Of this old mill town that I'll aye like the best.

Autumn has come now to my Teviot Valley,
Russet and gold leaves abound everywhere.
I walk through the park where the river runs gently
To tryst with the Slitrig its journey to share.
A tear dims my eye as I view the memorial,
Head bowed, I remember how Callants like me
Laid down their lives to ensure us our freedom
And lie now at Ypres and Gallipoli.

The snell wund it blusters across Teviot Valley
And brings frae the north land the sleet and the snaw.
The trees are all bare now, the days they are shorter,
The river is frozen and white Ruberslaw.
I hear the great storm as it blatters the window
But cosy I sit by my ain fireside.
I think of far lands where the sky will be golden
But thank God it's here in auld Hawick that I bide.

Then one day a gloamin descends on my valley
As dark shadows lengthen and evening comes still
I will be ready to take my last journey
To lie wi oor fithers on Wellogate's Hill
And if those who follow look after my valley
And cherish this auld toon sae precious to me
I'll rest in peace up above my green valley
For as long as the Teviot flows down to the sea.

Ian W. Landles. 26/27 March, 2004

Ian has produced a series of three books of portraits of 'Hawick's Honest Men and Bright Eyed Daughters' with his friend, photographer Derek Lunn. Here Ian portrays in the Teri dialect the characters of Hawick's well known faces.

William Landles

Photo: Derek Lunn

William 'Bill' Landles, artist and sculptor, is the third member of that creative clan we cannot fail to mention. Bill says he inherited his artistic ability from his father, Wull. Bill taught at Hawick High School, passing on his natural ability to countless pupils. As one of Scotland's finest sculptors, he is much in demand. Amongst Bill's work are the plaque erected on the 'The Hill Road To Roberton' to Will H. Ogilvie and the plaque of Adam Grant at 2 High Street, the site of Grant's first music shop. As we write, Bill is working on a statue to commemorate James Thomson, author and poet, who wrote such gems as "The Border Queen", "Hail to the Banner" and the song sung all over the world "The Star of Robbie Burns".

David Hill is perhaps the poet who best portrays the changing life in Hawick during the middle part of the century. He was able to paint mental pictures and convey the emotion and sense of loss of some familiar childhood landmarks and customs as the town drove forward the changes needed to embrace the prosperity and higher expectations of the Teri of the second part of the century. The truths of tales told

Cartoon of David Hill.

73

in works like "The Bleach", "Robbie Dye", and "Shundert" are reflected when read, on the faces of those who shared these times with him. No poem more so than

THE VERTISH

Ye may ken,
    I was born and bred i' The Loan.
In a yin-end whunstane biggin',
    Wi' an ootlook on to the Bleachin' Green
And Black-Brae craws on the riggin';
    A guid-gaun lum for a wunter's nicht,
Wi' my feet on the polished fender
    But they cam' and condemned it, and garred mei flit-
Mei! A born Wast-ender!
    I work away i' the spinnin' mill
Up to the cuits in ooder.
    But I'm fain for a sicht o' the Vertish Hill
Wi' his plaid flung owre his shooder.
    His waistcoat and breeks o' comely green,
The wud hei weers like a croon.
    And I mind o' the days that yince hae been
And my hert's sair cuissen-doon.
    For now o' The Loan that I used to ken
There's hardly a stannin' stane;
    Even my douce auld neebor The Moat
Looks muckle to mean and lane
    But hei has The Vertish to bield his back,
And keep things a' in order. . . .
    There's higher hills? Aye! But where'll ye sei
A bonnier view o' the Border?
    Man . . . Ocht worth tippence gaun on i' the toon
Aye comes there, sune or later-
    Comets and Callants and mairchin' bairns-
It's a local law o' Natur'!
    Golfers and sledgers and dydie-eggs,
Or auld folk seekin' a sate
    O' a simmer's nicht, the Hill's aye there
And his welcome never blate.
    So juist dinna let-on if ye sei mei nod

Guid-nicht, to my freend owre thonder
    As dowie I gang for the Burnfit bus
For mony's the time I ponder
    How is't that yon humphie-backit hicht
Can steer up thochts sae tender?
    For there's never a hill like the Vertish Hill
To a guitter-bluid Wast-ender!

Graham Murray. President of the Callants Club in 1997, made a substantial contribution to Border Literature and Poetry. Graham, following in a family tradition, was known by many for his brilliant performances as an orator and interpreter of other's poems. His delivery of the 'Epistle to Tammas', a poem by J.B. Selkirk made the whole tale live. Graham was also a gifted writer an example is

EWES AND TEVIOT
by J.Graham B.Murray

Throughout old Scotia's Border Grand
    From Solway's tide to Berwick stand,
Through varied scenes of Southern land
    Beyond the misty Cheviot,
To me no vision can compare
    In pastoral beauty rich and rare
With that which they together share
    The vales of Ewes and Teviot.

Linked are the twain at Old Mosspaul
    Where cadance of hill waterfall
Blends with the curlew's plaintiff call
    In telling of the lave o't,
Of cracking days when hostel gay
    Could sing a song or Border lay
To cheer the traveller on his way
    By winding Ewes and Teviot.

They tell of times in days of old
    When through these hills rode reivers bold
Their eager quest a well stocked fold
    Their purpose to relieve it!

We know that Jamie Telfer's kye
    By English loons were driven nigh
Returning homeward bye and bye
    Through vales of Ewes and Teviot

Changed now the scene and feudal line
    Gives place to prosperous peace divine,
A peace whose beauty heightens thine
    Sweet vales North of the Cheviot
Kind hearts beat true on ilka shore,
    Leal Border patriots to the core,
May theirs be long life to adore
    Their native Ewes and Teviot

It is difficult in a publication such as this to do justice to each and every art form. We have not covered dance or singers or indeed musicians, not even institutions like the Saxhorn Band or the P.S.A. Choir. We can but encourage the reader to seek out these performers and enjoy the talent abounding in our midst.

Brian Bonsor is one we cannot fail to mention. Principal Teacher of Music at Hawick High School and advisor at County then Regional Education levels he inspired many of his pupils to develop their musical talents. Brian was conductor of the Roxburgh Singers for many years and a prominent member of the Hawick Music Club. Since retiring from his school work Brian has built a world wide reputation teaching, promoting and holding workshops to develop the playing of the recorder. His publishing company Bonsor Music prints recorder music for both education and performance.

Photo: D. Lunn

76

The artist or painter is similarly not represented as they should be. A publication such as this cannot do true justice to reproductions of their work. Hawick has been fortunate to be the subject or home of some outstanding painters, **Tom Scott, RSA** (who was the first official guest at a Callants Club Dinner in 1906). **Anne Redpath** perhaps the most commercially successful.

R. E. (Dick) Scott (who also produced the book Companion to Hawick.) **Jack Young, Sandy Milligan, Moira** and **Stuart Beatty, Adam Robson,** Callants Club President in 2002, **John Miller, W.S.A., Ingles J. Miller** and many, many more.

A view of Selkirk by Tom Scott, RSA.

Children Playing in the Street, Anne Redpath.

Perhaps the most talked about artist in the borderland over the last century is Tom Scott, RSA. He has left us with a great legacy of his works, from all over the Borders, not least round about Hawick.

Anne Redpath is another whose work is much sought after. What a living story her oil on canvas of "Children Playing in the Street" tells.

Great scenes of Hawick and the surrounding area have been portrayed by many in water colour.

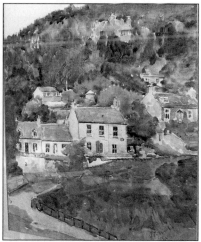

Wilton Dean, John Miller.

To do justice to the performing arts over the century would take a volume on its own. However one name stands out. That of **Jean Wintrope**, a leading performer with Hawick Operatic Society for many years before becoming their Producer. Her drive for perfection is legendary and can be seen in every performance of the Society. In the year 2000 through her 'Two Rivers Theatre Company' Jean produced to great acclaim, "The Gutterbluds" written by J E D Murray and Adam Grant. It is fitting perhaps that this performance should bring us full circle and demonstrate the continued creativity within Hawick.

Photo: D. Lunn

The reader will forgive the many omissions from this brief salute to those by whose creativity we in Hawick have been enriched.

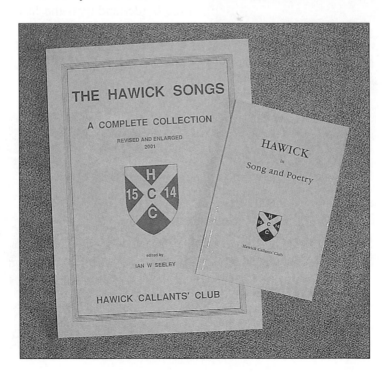

Common Riding and Cornets

Cornet D. Nuttall, 1939.

Compiled by
Ex-Cornet Carswell Imrie
David R H Nuttall

A COMMON RIDING CHRONOLOGY 1900–2004

This is a list of some of the significant events and changes relating to the Common Riding between 1900 and 2004, arranged by year. It is far from complete and quite subjective.

Compiled by Douglas Scott, David Nuttall, Ian Scott, Janet Scott and Bill Thomson, it makes use of a wide variety of sources and is essentially an update and extension of the Appendix in W. S. Robson's "Story of Hawick" (revised edition).

There are perhaps two lessons to be drawn from this list of changes: firstly, the Common Riding is a fluid entity, whose details evolve with time; but, secondly, the spirit of the Common Riding is strong and immutable enough to last it through these changes. The Common Riding of itself has "aye been", and has at its core a symbolism with the power to survive the adaptations which have been necessary to make it relevant for five centuries.

1900 Riding of the Marches moved to the Thursday morning.
First recorded Cornet's Lass and Chief Guest.
The Proclamations fully incorporated into the ceremonies. Commemorative plaque unveiled for James Hogg at 14 Loan on Common Riding Thursday.
First Mosspaul Ride-out.

1901 Curds and Cream repast held at Pilmuir for this year and the next ten. Flag returned to Hornshole (probably for the first time) for the unveiling of the Hornshole Monument.
"I Like Auld Hawick the Best" first sung at the Colour Bussing.

1902 "Up wi' Auld Hawick" and "Oor Bonnie Border Toon" first sung at the Colour Bussing.
Mrs. Oliver of Thornwood is the first female Chief Guest.

1903 New Flag made to match the original pennon shape with golden cross (rather than the square shape with red cross which had been in use from about 1832).
"Oor Ain Auld Toon" first sung at the Colour Bussing.

Ex-Cornet Darling stands in as Left-Hand Man, since Ex-Cornet Sutherland left for South Africa.

Hawick Callants Club formed on the 8th December.

1904 First year of Callants Club congratulatory Smoker for the Cornet.
Callants Club arrange for Flag to drape coffin of Ex-Cornet John Smith and this has since become a part of each Ex-Cornet's funeral.
Last year of the procession out to Bogliebarns.(Near to Millers Knowes entrance in Weensland Road)

1905 Riding of the Marches moves back to the Friday.
Drums and Fifes first escort the Cornet and his supporters from the Song Singing to the Town Hall.
Committee purchases three stones of lead for penalties in the Races.

1906 First year that a riding-crop presented to the Cornet.
First admission charge for the Colour Bussing.
The Drums and Fifes each given a shilling for transport to the Moor.
Race programmes first mentioned in the Committee minute books.

1907 Drums and Fifes get new uniforms (from Hume's at a cost of 45 shillings each), and three new fifes are purchased.
James Yule becomes official Song Singer.
Ca' Knowe Stakes and Saturday Plate instituted at the Races.
Cornet agrees not to arrive at the Moor until after the first race, to allow more time at Pilmuir.
Last time the Acting Father is the Cornet's real father.
First time "The Anvil Crew" sung at the Colour Bussing.

1908 Common Riding committees reorganised, with main Committee of twenty-two members appointed by the Council. As a result the celebrations are much more under municipal control than previously.
Committee vote against a request to repeat the Common Riding ceremonies at the Scottish National Exhibition in Edinburgh.
Flag loaned for consecration ceremony of Hexham Priory's new nave.

1909 "Bonnie Teviotdale" and "The Fairest Spot o' A'" first sung at the Colour Bussing.
Special train runs from Newcastle on the Saturday.

1910 Riding of the Marches is moved to the Saturday.
Drums and Fifes first play during the singing of "Teribus" at the Common Riding.
First singing of "Hawick" with current tune at the Colour Bussing.

1911 "The Banner Blue" first sung at the Colour Bussing.
Will Ogilvie has to cancel his attendance at Colour Bussing due to the sudden death of his sister, and Rev. D. Cathels stood in.
Ex-Cornet Glendinning also stands in as Left-Hand Man for Ex-Cornet Scott due to a bereavement.
Amateur Games moved to the Friday and Professional Games to the Saturday.
Coronation Cup donated for the winner of the Tradesmen's Handicap.
Duke of Buccleuch gifts most of Mote Park to the Town.
Ca' Knowe cairn erected by the Callants Club.

1912 Curds and Cream moved permanently to St. Leonard's.
Presentation at the Colour Bussing to Andrew Ballantyne for 60 years of service as a drummer.
Games changed back to Professional on Friday, Amateur on Saturday.

1913 Games are switched between Friday and Saturday once again.

1914 The Quater-Centenary year.
Special Vertish Hill Sports on the Saturday before the Common Riding, with a procession of about 3,600 children led by the Cornet and 15 mounted supporters.
The Kirking ceremony combined with the celebration of the 700th anniversary of the consecration of St. Mary's, with about 4,000 people cramming into the churchyard.
The 1514 Memorial (The Horse) unveiled.
Two performances of a historical pageant held in the Volunteer Park on the Tuesday and Wednesday.
Two separate Colour Bussing ceremonies carried out.
Riding of the Marches moved back to Friday.
Copy of the Flag presented to Hexham Abbey by the Callants Club.

1915 Common Riding cancelled because of the Great War.
The Council and the Callants Club resolve to do nothing, but J.E.D.

Murray rides the marches on his own.
Vertish Hill Sports held on Common Riding Friday.
Well discovered at the Paddock.

1918 Common Riding weekend used for Red Cross benefit events and the Vertish Hill Sports held on the Saturday.

1919 First Common Riding after WW I.
No licensed tents on the Moor for the first time, with Temperance marquee doing great business.
Bus crashes at the Vertish returning from the Moor, four people killed.
Two separate Colour Bussing ceremonies carried out.
Song-Singing ceremony temporarily moved to the Horse.
Hamilton B. Little becomes the official Song Singer.

1920 Two separate Colour Bussing ceremonies again carried out.
Volunteer Park purchased.
The Ancient Order of Mosstroopers' reconstituted, having existed from the early 1900s; one of its main aims is to encourage mounted supporters to follow the Cornet.

1921 Song Singer first takes charge of the Snuffing.
Riding of the Marches switched again to the Thursday morning.
Presentation at the Colour Bussing to James Douglas for 50 years as a drummer.

1922 Presentation at the Colour Bussing to Andrew Ballantyne for 70 years service as a drummer.

1923 First year of "bussing" the flag on the Horse monument, i.e. tying ribbons on the Thursday night. Cornet also lowers the Flag while passing the Horse during the Friday Procession.
New rules at the Races, stating that winners of ten pound races must have accompanied the Cornet on the Thursday and Saturday of the week prior to the Common Riding.

1924 Opening of "The Hut" by Provost J. Renwick, J. Renwick Jnr being Cornet.
First year of 'bussing' the flag on the 1514 Memorial (Horse monument).

New rules at the Races, introducing qualifying races stating that horses must have accompanied the Cornet on the Thursday and Saturday of the week prior to the Common Riding.

1925 J.E.D. Murray is Acting Father for the fourth and last time.
Arrangement for the Drums and Fifes to play the Cornet from the Town Hall to the Horse on the Thursday Night, and the Saxhorn Band to play him back after the Cornet's Walk.
Increase of allowance for Cornet to 75 pounds and Right- and Left-Hand Men to 12 pounds 10 shillings each.

1926 Cornet's Silver Challenge Cup prize money increases and a gold medal instituted.

1927 Medway Cup (presented by Oliver Kennedy) replaces the Branxholm Stakes.
Marjorie Haddon (perhaps the first female jockey) rides in this race on the Saturday.

1928 Loud speakers introduced outside the Town Hall at the Colour Bussing.

1929 Responsibility for stabling of the Prinicipals' horses taken over by the Council.

1930 New set of drums and fifes provided by Oliver Hardie and T.M. Hardie in the centenary year of their grandfather's Cornetship.
"Hawick in Song and Poetry" first published by the Callants Club.

1932 Presentation to Andrew Ballantyne Anderson at the Colour Bussing, for fifty years service in the Drums and Fifes.
Totalisator introduced for betting at the Races this year only.

1933 Colour Bussing held in the Volunteer Park.

1934 Colour Bussing broadcast on radio by the BBC.
Common Riding moved back to the Friday.
Another revival of the canter out to Bogliebarns before the Friday morning Chase.
Presentation to John Anderson at the Colour Bussing for fifty years as a fifer.

1936 First Overseas Night.
Last year of the procession to Bogliebarns.
Coronation Cup won outright.

1937 New rules for the Mosstroopers' Stakes.
Duke of Buccleuch gives the Ca' Knowe site and access path to the town.

1938 J.E.D. Murray Trophy presented.

1939 Saturday races are changed to start at 11.15 a.m.
New rule debarring from the Races any horse winning two cash prizes of 4 pounds or more.

1940 Common Riding cancelled during the Second World War.
The marches are ridden by Ex-Cornet Chap Landles, accompanied by some supporters.

1945 Jim Reid appointed Battalion Cornet by the K.O.S.B., using a flag made by the women of Pringle's.
"Hawick in Song and Poetry" re-issued as the "Red Book".

1946 First Common Riding after the War.
The Cornet of 1937, W. Lockie Thorburn, is Right-Hand Man for the second time, while the Cornet of 1935, Bill Brydon, is Left-Hand Man again.
Bottom corner of the race-course improved.

1947 Andrew Ballantyne Anderson and his brother John Anderson retire after, respectively, 64 and 62 years in the Drums and Fifes. Band get R.A.F. uniforms dyed navy blue.

1950 Rufus Trophy won outright and replaced with the Hornshole Stakes.

1951 Riders issued with cards to enter Ride-out attendance as qualification for the Races.
Hornshole and Mosstroopers' Stakes interchanged, as well as the Medway Stakes and Teri Stakes.
Horrific accident during the Municipal Handicap when three riders fall, and one later dies in hospital.

1955 Thursday morning riding attendance removed as a qualification for the races.

Medway stakes becomes the first Cornet's race on the Friday.

J.E.D. Murray Trophy moved to the Saturday.

Ex-Cornets first asked to pay for Ball tickets.

1956 Learmonth Stakes discontinued.

Oliver Hogg becomes the first local rider to win the Tradesmen's Handicap.

1957 First brooch presented to Cornet's Lass at Colour Bussing, with all surviving Lasses also receiving a brooch.

1959 New Cornet's Sash made by hosiery apprentices at the Henderson Technical College.

1961 Amateur Games discontinued on the Friday.

Centre gallery at the Colour Bussing reserved solely for "the Lads".

1963 First time the Acting Father takes charge of the Flag during the wreath-laying ceremony at the War Memorial on Common-Riding Saturday.

Ladies toilets built at the Paddock.

1964 Extensions to "the Hut".

Rule prescribing that dinner jackets be worn at the Ball.

Cornet no longer attends Volunteer Park Games on the Saturday.

Letter of thanks to the Misses McCallum, Old Manse, Myreslawgreen in recognition of 70 years of service in distributing refreshments to the riders.

Release of volume 1 of "Songs of Hawick" record, sponsored by the Callants'Club.

Hawick Film Group's "Sons of Heroes" made, including scenes from this year's Common Riding.

1965 Release of 2nd volume of "Songs of Hawick".

1972 Replacement Flag presented to Hexham Abbey by the Provost.

1973 Bert Armstrong becomes official Song Singer.
First year of an allowance for the Cornet's Lass (25 pounds).
Professional security company employed for the first time at the
Races.

1975 First Common Riding without a formal Town Council.

1977 New constitution of the Common Riding Committee after local
government reorganisation.
Hon.Provosts Council formed and constituted at a Public meeting
following proposals made by Callants Club.
The Hon.Provost and Baillies wear 'The Robes' for Ceremonial duties
at the Common-Riding and Remembrance Day Parades.
Constitution of 1514 Club formalised; the Club having been formed
around 1961.
Cornets Lass lays her wreath at Hornshole Memorial on Kirking
Sunday for the first time. Previously done on the Thursday night after
the Colour-Bussing.

1978 Revised "Hawick in Song and Poetry" (the Blue Book) published by
the Callants Club.

1986 "Hawick Sings" recording released by the 1514 Club.

1987 Cairn erected by the 1514 Club to mark the Burnford, i.e. the closest
point of Hawick's Common. Second volume of "Hawick Sings"
released.

1988 Myra Turnbull becomes the first female Honorary Provost.
Henry Douglas becomes official Song Singer.
Games no longer run by the Common Riding Committee.
Last year of the Secondary Ball.

1990 Drums and Fifes receive new uniforms.

1992 New Flag presented by C.N. Whillans.

1993 Rules changed allowing Cornet to be born outside Hawick, provided
birth is registered in Hawick by parents living in Hawick.

Instigation of poetry competition for 1st year High School pupils in memory of Jack Murray.

1994 Plaques placed to mark the position of the four tolls, which feature in the Cornet's Walk.

1996 Lady Riders Dispute - Cornets Ride out to Denholm on the Saturday before the Common Riding saw hostile scenes as four girls tried to join the cavalcade.
There followed a year of bitter dispute with the matter being taken to Court.
The episode caused great division in the town and did untold damage to Hawick's reputation throughout the world.

1997 Women officially allowed on two Rides-out and Common Riding Saturday.

1998 Highland dancing moved from the Volunteer to the Moor.

1999 Adam Grant Memorial at 6 High Street unveiled on the Sunday of the Kirking.

2000 Michael Aitken becomes official Song Singer.
Highland dancing dropped entirely.
Mosstroopers' Club erect a cairn at Mosspaul.

2001 Common Riding cancelled because of foot and mouth outbreak. Previous year's Principals lead a walk in November, after the countryside ban is lifted.
Third edition of "Hawick in Song and Poetry" (the Green Book) published by the Callants Club.

2002 Flag bussed by the Queen in Melrose as part of the Golden Jubilee celebrations.
Cornet's Walk held immediately after Colour Bussing to encourage more participants, before ribbons tied at the Horse.

2003 Horse monument moved several feet as part of traffic re-routing. Drum presented to the Drums and Fifes by the Scott family in memory of the late Frank Scott.

2004 Acting Mother becomes an official title.

First time the Cornet's Dinner is a mixed event and chaired by a female, Hon. Provost Zandra Elliot

Ceremonial and General Committees merged.

Hawick Callants Club centenary.

Hawick Common Riding, 1902. The Cornet was William N. Graham, plumber.

Cornet D. Nuttall, 1939.

Hawick Ex-Cornets and Acting Fathers, June 1948

Back Row l to r: C. N. Whillans, 1948. C. Bell, 1946. D. Nuttall, 1939. Wm. Brydon, 1935. W. L. Thorburn, Jnr., 1937. J. H. Haig, 1936. J. Martin, 1938. R. V. Scott, 1947. G. Peden (AF), 1948.

Third Row l to r: J. E. Graham, 1933. R. Pringle (AF), 1947. J. M. Ballantyne (AF), 1935. A. R. Innes, 1931. G. Wilson, 1932. W. A. Mactaggart, 1930. R. C. Appleby (AF), 1937. G. B. Hall, 1934. J. B. Elliot (AF), 1939. G. Ormiston (AF), 1946.

Second Row l to r: J. Rae, 1923. J. Haig (AF), 1933. R. E. Tait, 1920. G. H. Armstrong (AF), 1932. J. D. Bonsor, 1912. I. G. Wallis (AF), 1931. J. C. Landles, 1921. C. K. Morton (AF), 1934. G. D. Scott, 1925.

Front Row l to r: R. Baxter (AF), 1929. J. Glendining, 1908. G. L. McDonald (AF), 1906, 1930. W. E. Kyle, 1905. F. Park, 1897. P. H. Robertson, 1899. G. Davidson (AF), 1913. W. L. Thorburn, 1911. C. W. Grieve (AF), 1919, 1927.

Cornet 1952.

Sheila MacDonald, 1948.

Cornets Lass, 1971.

Cornets Lass, 2002.

Cornets Lass, 1950

Cornets Lass, 1961.

Lasses, 1952.

Greta Reid, 1946.

Cornet and Lass, 1947.

Helen Hall, 1966.

Hawick Common Riding, 1967

Quater-Centenary Plate.

BOOK SIGNED BY EACH CORNET AND ACTING FATHER

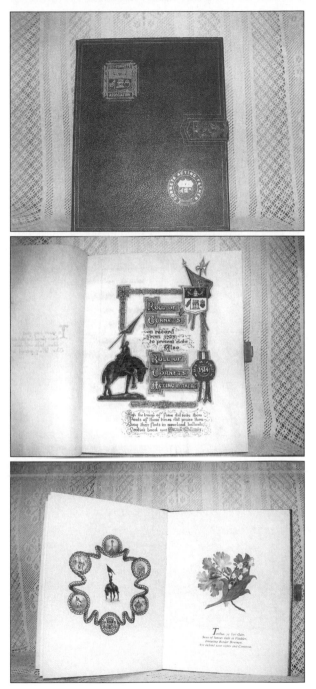

Bonchester Ride-out, 1948.

Mosspaul Ride-out, 1951.
F. Borthwick, J. M. Richardson, A. Cavers, J. Berkley, at the rear D. Nuttall.

Cutting the sod, 1956.
Ex-Acting Father T. Crosby, Ex-Cornet T. Thomson, O. Hogg, Cornet Robert B. Fraser,
Acting Father E. Tait, Ex-Cornet Bruce Mactaggart, W. Amos, Ex-Acting Father J. Leithead

Cornet, 1994.

Photo: Lesley Fraser

Cornet, 1999.

Photo: Lesley Fraser

Cornet, 2003.

Photo: Lesley Fraser

Cornet, 1996.

Cornet, 2000.

YEAR	CORNET	ACTING FATHER	CORNET'S LASS
1900	F Park	A W Kerr	Agnes Reid
1901	J Sutherland	J E D Murray	Lily Lawson
1902	W Graham	H Anderson	Margaret K Drummond
1903	W E Scott	M Dechan	Lunn
1904	G Scott	G Scott	Janet Riddle
1905	W E Kyle	J E D Murray	Jean Elliott
1906	J W S Robertson	C L McDonald	Mary Sutherland
1907	T Jardine	Thomas Jardine	Agnes Robson
1908	J Glendinning	Henderson	Elizabeth Thomson
1909	T Scott	R Inglis	Jane Haig
1910	A D Haddon	Conn	Gladys Laidlaw
1911	W L Thorburn	Payne	Barbara Pringle
1912	J D Bonsor	J E D Murray	A M Wilson
1913	R Elder	G Davidson	N Guy
1914	G Wilson	A Laing	Elizabeth Turnbull
1919	T G Winning	C W Grieve	M Davidson
1920	R I Tait	J D Bonsor	Dorothy Harvey
1921	J C G Landles	Col. Kennedy	Bessie Irvine
1922	F Henderson	A H Robertson	I Johnstone
1923	J Rae	D Fenwick	Bella Elder
1924	J Renwick	A D Haddon	Isabella Rutherford
1925	G D Scott	J E D Murray	Ella Christie
1926	T P Allison	Dr Davidson	Marjory Haddon
1927	J Glenny	C W Grieve	Rosemary Wilson
1928	I G Mactaggart	J D Bonsor	Margaret Henderson
1929	R A V Grieve	R Baxter	Jean D Elliott
1930	W A Mactaggart	G L McDonald	M Innes
1931	A R Innes	I G Wallace	Elizabeth Pringle
1932	G Wilson	G M Armstrong	Emily Graham
1933	J Graham	Jas Haig	Elsie Carruthers
1934	G Hall	C K Morton	Myra Irvine

CALLANTS CLUB PRESIDENT	MOSSTROOPERS PRESIDENT	1514 Club PRESIDENT
Tom Kerr		
Ex-Baillie Dechan		
A H Drummond		
W T Grieve		
A R Oliver		
J E D Murray		
Dr W T Barrie		
J G Winning		
Provost Melrose		
A S Lawson		
W A Innes		
Baillie Scott		
J R Purdom	T G Winning	
G L McDonald	R E Tait	
J S Turner	J C G Landles	
J Hobkirk	F Henderson	
J Edgar	J Rae	
Provost Renwick	J Renwick	
Sir T Henderson	J E D Murray	
W E Kyle	P Allison	
A D Haddon	Col. Kennedy	
J Marshall	J D Bonsor	
G Gass	W E Kyle	
T D Elliott	W E Kyle	
G Davidson	G A Scott	
J C Bonsor	I G Mactaggart	
J Glendinning	G H Armstrong	

1935	W Brydon	J Ballantyne	Jean Butler
1936	H Haig	S Drummond Miller	Jeanette Wilson
1937	L Thorburn	R C Appleby	Grace Veitch
1938	J P Martin	J Rae	Elizabeth Tait
1939	D Nuttall	J B Elliott	Effie Wood
1946	C Bell	D Ormiston	Greta Reid
1947	Bert Scott	R Pringle	Margaret Collier
1948	C N Whillans	G Peden	Sheila MacDonald
1949	W Cavers	J Henderson	Della Oliver
1950	T Crosby	M Buchan	Grace Miller
1951	G Aitken	T I Storrie	Helen Allan
1952	J Wright	Ex.C. D Nuttall	Ella Crozier
1953	J Turnbull	T College	Mary Bowie
1954	B Mactaggart	Ex.C. J Martin	Maureen Simpson
1955	T Thomson	W G Robertson	Isla Marchbank
1956	R Fraser	E Tait	Irene Kennedy
1957	D Lunn	G Hardie	Eileen Johnstone
1958	J Nuttall	G A Scott	Myra Elliott
1959	N Murray	S Gardener	Evelyn Armstrong
1960	J Huggan	J Leithead	Eileen Wylie
1961	N Dickey	T Crosby	Christine Anderson
1962	B Patterson	F Baillie	Joan Grieve
1963	J Hope	J C Leithead	Lillian Young
1964	R Brydon	A L Ingles	Sheila Deans
1965	R Pringle	W F Hutton	Kathleen Peden
1966	C Imrie	J Lyle	Helen Hall
1967	G Peden	Ex.C. C N Whillans	Valerie Leithead
1968	J E Hutton	J Robertson	Sheila Richardson
1969	B G Wilson	A Armstrong	Valerie Franklin
1970	R K Gibson	W Scott	Vivienne Young
1971	D Martin	Ex.C B Mactaggart	Joyce Robson
1972	A P Murray	T Hogg	Ruth Crosby
1973	G Turnbull	A Stevenson	Lynda Elliott

M Scott	G Wilson
A J Grieve	J E Graham
G Cairns	J Henderson
J Forbes	A R Innes
J Park	D C Scott
R Hunter	D C Scott
D A Ross Haddon	C K Morton
R Baxter	D Nuttall
A R Innes	C Bell
Jas Haig	J Scott
W A Mactaggart	J Peden
G H Armstrong	R V Scott
W A Davidson	J M Buchan
C D Scott	W E Cavers
I G Mactaggart	J Murray
W Park	G Aitken
B P Ellis	G Hardie
G Wilson	C N Whillans
J P Martin	D N Smith
D Nuttall	T N Crosby
W G R Robertson	A Bouglas
A W Stenhouse	J C Leithead
W E Kyle	F Baillie
C S Baxter	J Nuttall
J T Peacock	D Dickson
E Tait	A E Cavers
T Marchbank	A L Ingles
J S Irvine	N Dickey
Dr A Simpson	G Wright
John Graham	D Lunn
R V Scott	J Arnot
Murray Aitken	J Lyle
C N Whillans	Ex.C. J D Robertson

1974	R Knox	A Buchan	Shirley Campbell
1975	C McCrerie	B Muir	Helen Hume
1976	H L Hinton	J Yallop	Anne Sanderson
1977	J D Robertson	J Thomson	Moira Johnstone
1978	D Inglis	H Douglas	Maureen Lunn
1979	D Brown	A Cowan	Margaret McLeod
1980	B T Campbell	J Turnbull	Carol Fraser
1981	D Blacklock	T Hartop	Morag Guthrie
1982	T Smith	W Gray	Marion Dickson
1983	J G Hogg	A M Graham	Margaret Rorrison
1984	I T Nichol	Ex.C. N Dickey	Lesley Millar
1985	I Whillans	S Barker	Sandra Mole
1986	D Nuttall	W H Wear	Gael Taylor
1987	E Turnbull	I Armstrong	Jackie Fletcher
1988	S Farish	I Young	Linda Falconer
1989	J Douglas	Ex.C. R Pringle	Gaye Dyer
1990	C Murray	R Duff	Sandra Wallace
1991	G Scott	R Charters	Jackie Hope
1992	C Niblo	J Hogg	Georgina Jackson
1993	R Culton	M Richardson	Elizabeth Fraser
1994	R Pringle	I Fraser	Loris Szoneberg
1995	L Matthews	P Nichol	Angela Gray
1996	A Wear	G Paxton	Julie Hodgins
1997	S Irvine	N Turnbull	Gillian Patterson
1998	R Walker	Ex.C. John Hope	Lynda Jackson
1999	G Young	C Thorburn	Katie Short
2000	B Richardson	K McCartney	Kirsty Tait
2001	Foot and Mouth	Foot and Mouth	Foot and Mouth
2002	S Anderson	L Marshall	R Jardine
2003	Greg McLeod	D Whillans	Laura Armstong
2004	C Rodgerson	Ian Reid	Amy Warden

D Dickson	W G Robertson	
T N Crosby	G Peden	
A L Ingles	J Hope	
W B Mactaggart	B Patterson	J Blackie
R Hunter	J Short	R Murphy
A Armstrong	W Scott	R Tait
J Nuttall	T Thomson	J Yallop
L Redpath	B Mactaggart	A Buchan
W Turnbull	J Yallop	N Turnbull
D Lunn	R Murray	H Douglas
W R Scott	T Hogg	J Tait
Dr A R Simpson	A E R Gordon	J Beattie
J Robertson	A P Murray	R Charters
D N Smith	A P Stevenson	T Froud
N Murray	J Hogg	J Mathews
F T Scott	H Douglas	H Simpson
G Penman	N J Turnbull	K McCartney
J Aitken	J Tait	I M Landles
R Pringle	W Bell	J Hogg
G Peden	W Wear	T Hartop
A Philip Murray	J Robertson	R Nichol
P J P Miller	S Culton	A Pow
T Hogg	M Richardson	G Paxton
J G B Murray	H Innes	J Robertson
G Malcolm Murray	E Hope	I Reid
R W Laidlaw	J MacPherson	M Aitken
D R H Nuttall	A Smith	C Murray
J A Buchan	S Marshall	I Nichol
A Robson	S Lambie	B Smith
R W Muir	F Scott	G Harrow
T M Hartop	G Jackson	J Tait

Hawick and its Wars

Compiled by
James M Coltman
James Anderson

The Great War

WAR! Nothing makes a bigger impact on a community than being at war and, in its one hundred year existence; Hawick Callants Club has witnessed two world wars and many smaller conflicts.

The following will give some idea of the way our town was affected by these historic times. We will not dwell upon the military aspect, but rather the way ordinary life was affected in the town.

The aim is to encourage some of our older citizens to recall events and times, some sad, some memorable, that shaped their lives and we hope that it will stimulate the young amongst us, to seek more information and learn from the sacrifices of previous generations.

The first war after the formation of the Callants Club was, of course, the Great or First World War of 1914-18. The people of Hawick played a great part in this, especially the young men, many of whom made the supreme sacrifice of giving their lives. In common with other communities, the town lost almost a generation of young callants at places like Gallipoli, Paschendale and Ypres.

We would like to recommend, especially to the young, the reading of the book "Hawick and the Great War", available at Hawick Library and Museum.

7th & 8th Service Battalion Colour

A company of Belgian refugees who arrived at Sillerbithall on 8th January, 1915.

Hawick National Reserves paraded at the Drill Hall, 20th August, 1914.
Lt.-Col. Haddon is shown reading the conditions of service to the men.

Hawick Territorials and National Reservists photographed at Galapark School, Galashiels.

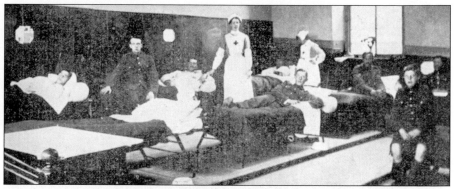

A corner of one of the wards in the military hospital, Trinity School.

A group of wounded Hawick soldiers home on furlough.
Back: Sam Hogg (K.O.S.B.), George Herbert (2nd Dragoons),
Peter Richardson (2nd K.O.S.B.), David Douglas (R.A.M.C.),
Lce.-Cpl. H. Redpath (K.O.S.B.)
Middle: Driver George Smith (A.S.C.), Sergt. A. Eckford (2nd K.O.S.B.),
Pte. J. Hume (2nd K.O.S.B.),Cpl. R. Anderson (A.S.C.), Lce.-Cpl. Wm. Boyd (2nd K.O.S.B.)
Front: Fred Cumming (2nd K.O.S.B.),Bombardier Jason Duncan (R.F.A.),
Bugler W. Berridge (2nd K.O.S.B.)

The Soldiers' Institute in the Baptist church hall.

"Flower Day" organised by Miss Laidlaw, Hazelwood, in aid of the Belgian Relief Fund, which realised over £124.

Flag Day in aid of the Scottish Women's Field Hospitals. This Flag Day was arranged by the Hawick Women's Suffrage Society and, after paying expenses, £100 was handed to Dr. Elsie Inglis on behalf of the object named.

Comforts for Hawick Prisoners of War in Germany.
A weekly dispatch from the Municipal Buildings to POWs in Germany. The picture affords
abundant evidence that the prisoners were well remembered.

A selection of World War I embroidered cards sent home by serving soldiers.

Sailors' Flag Day in Hawick.

Lieut.-General Sir F. J. Davies, K.C.B., K.C.M.G., K.C.V.O., G.O.C. Scottish Command and Provost Melrose, taking the salute.

The Second World War

THE SECOND WORLD WAR made an even bigger impact on the town as everyone was involved in some way, either by being "called-up" on National Service for the duration of the hostilities, or being in some war-time occupation such as munitions or coal mining or, as many women were, to work on the land in the Women's Land Army.

The town saw many changes. With Stobs Camp being so near, the town was virtually a garrison town. This meant many nationalities temporarily being billeted here, many marrying local girls or returning after the war. We also had German and Italian prisoners, displaced persons and Polish servicemen, as can be witnessed by some of the more unusual and surprising names to be found here and in the surrounding towns.

"Kent faces" in a group of "Terriers" who joined up before war began.

"Dads Army" – The Home Guard.

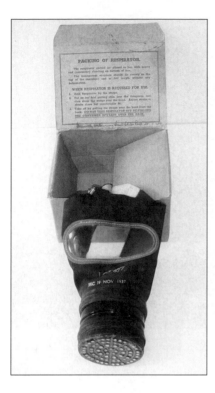

PACKING OF RESPIRATOR.

The respirator should be placed in box with heavy and (container) closing on bottom of box.

The transparent eyepiece should be coming on the top of the container and all but length without any deterioration.

WHEN RESPIRATOR IS REQUIRED FOR USE.

1. Hold Respirator by the straps.
2. Put an (by) face putting chin into the (container) and then draw the straps over the head. Adjust straps to make them feel comfortable fit.
3. Take off by pulling the straps over the head from the back. DO NOT TAKE RESPIRATOR OFF BY PULLING THE CONTAINER UPARD OVER THE FACE.

This little maid is prepared for any eventually.

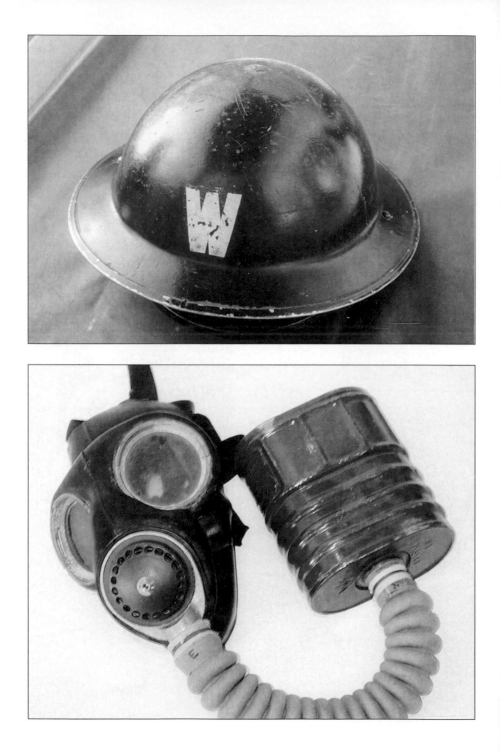

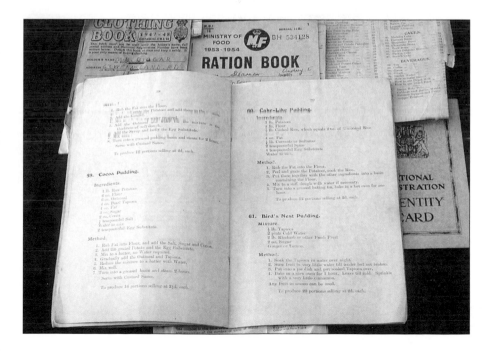

The first baby's gas mask to reach Hawick being "tried out" at Trinity School.

Car headlamp dimmer for blackout.

Land Army girls on parade during "Wings for Victory" week.

The Spitfire for which Hawick subscribed £5324 in five weeks.

Scientifically Built for · ACTIVE SERVICE

Athletic, streamlined, never bunches, never rides-up . . . .
Haven't you often found — especially when doing active work — that your underwear bunches and rides-up and irritates you?

That never happens with Y-Front underwear—it keeps everything perfectly in place all day. The vests are actually contoured to the figure so that they cannot wrinkle or ride-up. Best of all, the Y-Front masculine support takes the strain off important

muscles. You feel less tired at the end of the day

In addition to these factors it is good to remember that Y-Fronts show the result of a scientific approach to this age-old problem of men's underwear. Here we illustrate all styles in Y-Fronts and the range is compiled to offer you just the amount of coverage you personally require, whatever the season. Prices range from 4/9 to 16/6

VESTS, SHORTS, MID-WAYS, LONGS

Coopers Y-front UNDERWEAR

LYLE & SCOTT, LTD., HAWICK, SCOTLAND
London Office—IDEAL HOUSE, ARGYLL ST., LONDON, W.I.

SAVE EVERY SCRAP OF SCRAP

An urgent call is made for **WASTE PAPER.** Books, letters, old documents, wrapping paper, newspapers; indeed every kind of wastepaper is wanted NOW. Do your bit. Small quantities should be tied in bundles and put out alongside your dustbin. If you have large quantities 'phone the Town Clerk's Office— and it will be collected

Waste Materials are War Materials

BURGH OF HAWICK

Life went on – people got married, babies were born, food was grown and industry carried on. People still socialised and played sport and the Common was still marked, although in a subdued way.

Money was raised and parcels sent to prisoners of war via the Red Cross.

Hawick men serving with the 4th KOSB even managed to hold Common Ridings each June, the last being held in the East German town of Letzlingen, for which a replica flag was made by the young lasses of Pringle Ltd. and sent out to the men in time for June 1945.

The "colts" keep the rugby game alive during wartime. Snap taken at a match between Pringles and the BB.

4th Hawick BB won the Beattie Shield and the Championship at the BB Sports.

COMMON-RIDING, 1941

"_The Cornet and his merry men_
On 'METAL' steeds are prancing"

Ex-Provost Landles and his cavalcade on the racecourse after the Riding of the Marches at this year's "token" Common Riding.

Ex-Provost Landles heading the "token" Common Riding procession.

The Common Riding flag made by the girls of Robert Pringles & Son for the KOSB boys in Germany.

Bathing belles at a garden party at Ardlui.

More women are taking to bowling on Wilton Lodge Park.

Snap of Fusilier W. D. Giles, Stobs, and Brydon Hood of the RAMC. Teries who met in the Middle East.

Countess of Minto with Mr Walter Cranston and Mr E. McQuaid at an "Aid for Russia" demonstration.

Girl voluntary workers doing their bit of National Service by sewing blankets.

Scene on the Vertish Hill at the Children's Sports.

The Countess of Minto packed the 100,000th parcel to be sent out from the Red Cross Parcels Depot at Hawick since the war began.

1st September, 1942.
Robert Barbour, Esq.,
 Town Clerk,
  HAWICK.

Dear Mr. Barbour,

I thank you for your letter of 27th August with reference to medical supplies. I presume you are referring only to the town of Hawick, and as far as I am aware (although my only official position is in connection with the Home Guard) you have the, First Aid Post at Trinity School, with the Casualty Hospital at the Cottage Hospital, and there are three Collecting Stations - Springbank Clinic, the Casual Ward at Drumlanrig Home, and the Forresters Hall, O'Connell Street, There are also the mobile ambulances ready to deal with casualties when called to any point.

I am not quite clear as to what you mean as to the invasion occurring, because in the event of a blitz, that is to say a bombing of Hawick, a Company of the Home Guard, with all the stretcher-bearers and myself are stationed at a strategic point (Wellogate) to be able to deal with Home Guard casualties, but in the event of Hawick itself being invaded then I have to retire to the British Legion Canteen which becomes the Regimental Aid post, and as the First Aid Post and Cottage Hospital are outside the Area, practically speaking all the casualties would have to be attended to there. There is of course the Hall opposite which would be an overflow in the event of such an occurrence.

I may say the medical men know exactly what they have to do in the event of an invasion, and where they are to be i.e. Dr. Scott, assisted by Dr. Milne, at the Cottage Hospital, Dr. Haddon, assisted by Dr. Henderson, at the First Aid Post, while I am with the Home Guard either on duty in the area, or in the Regimental Aid Post in the British Legion Canteen.

I may say that at the try-out recently held during the night the Canteen was used for evacuation of all Home Guard casualties and the whole proceedings worked very satisfactorily.

There are ample supplies of course scattered about in the various chemists' shops, etc. which would be made available in the event of anything occurring, not to mention the doctors' houses, and other sundry posts.

It is a little difficult, not having fortunately contacted any of the blitz stuff to visualise just exactly what might be required, but I think the existing arrangements are reasonably satisfactory.

All the Home Guard medical equipment is kept in the interim in the First Aid Room at the Drill Hall, and the ambulance which is to be at the disposal of the Home Guard for carting my gear about is in the S.M.T.Garage at Dovecote Street, so that everything is near to our Battalion Headquarters for easy access.

If there are any other points that I can help you with I would be glad, but I feel probably Mr. Cairns of the A.R.P. would be better able to tell you the minor medical supply depots in the Area.

Yours truly,
A.Simpson (Dr)

First in the queue.

17th February, 1943.

FOLLOWING ARE A FEW WEDDING PICTURES OF WEEL KENT FACES, SOME WHO CAME AND STAYED AND ONE WHO WENT AWAY.

Captain James R. Scott-Noble and Miss Diana Dickson.

Miss M. Grierson, Renwick Terrace and Cpl. W. Potter, RM.

Miss Margaret Froud, Ramsay Road and Sergt-Maj. J. G. Boyd, a former "Greens" three-quarter.

Miss Margaret Hay, 1 Slitrig Place and Gunner Edward Howlett, Canadian Royal Army.

Cpl. Lloyd English, USA and LACW Margaret Fisher

A glimpse of Dickson Street on VE day.

Typical of the German prisoners working on our housing sites.

Hawick's "pre-fabs" at Silverbuthall.

How Hawick celebrated "VJ" day – street dancing with Saxhorn Band playing at the Tower Knowe, while fireworks were bursting in High Street.

Here are stalwart Guardsmen leading Hawick's Victory Parade, which included all the Civil Defence Services and voluntary organisations who had played their part in the war effort.

AND AT LONG LAST – IT ENDED!

The fallen of the two world wars were remembered at this year's Armistice Day Service at the Memorial in Wilton Lodge Park.

Remembering the Centenary of the unveiling of the Boer War Memorial
(l to r) Bugler C. Crozier, Major L. Godfrey, Provost Z. Elliot,
Major J. Aitken, M.B.E., T.D., C.A., Piper J. Coltman
2003.

Many thanks to Hawick Museum, Mr David Hill and Mr William Thomson for the photographs.

Sporting Heroes

Compiled by
Brian King
Ronnie Hodgins
John M Hamilton

Local Sporting Heroes

Over the past 100 years the town of Hawick has produced many fine sportsmen and women, not only at world and international level, but domestically and in all categories of sport.

In the post war years, and before, there were many 'back street' breeding grounds in neighborhoods throughout the town where raw and inherent talent was much in evidence. Without the distractions of television and computers, there was probably greater emphasis on outdoor activities as a means of self-entertainment and more opportunity to emulate the feats and triumphs of those sporting stars of the times – the perfect place to nurture champions of the future.

This selection of 'Heroes' cannot be a comprehensive coverage of those who have represented our Town with distinction. All we can hope is that our choices stimulate discussion and brings recognition to Hawick's outstanding sporting talent in the Twentieth Century.

BILL McLAREN, M.B.E, O.B.E., C.B.E.

Britain's most respected and best loved commentator and known simply as 'the voice of rugby'. Bill retired from the BBC in 2002 to complete a broadcasting career spanning 50 years which earned him worldwide admiration.

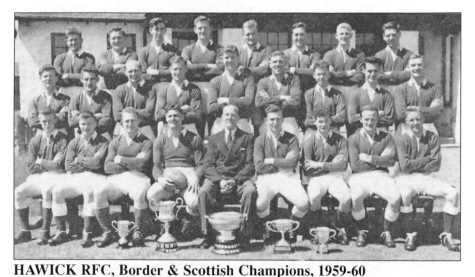

HAWICK RFC, Border & Scottish Champions, 1959-60

The 1959–60 Greens, known as 'Jack Hegarty's Team', perhaps one of the finest of all Hawick sides who were described as being 'ahead of their time' for their style of play.
Back row left to right: E. W. Broatch, T. S. Barker, R. Valentine, T. O. Grant,
D. Murray, J. Cunningham, B. King, A. R. Broatch.
Middle: R. J. Grieve, J. Wallace, A. Robson, G. D. Stevenson, W. J. Hunter, R. B. Brydon,
C. Renwick, T. Edmison, D. Grant.
Front: W. D. Jackson, J. H. Gray. H. F. McLeod, J. J. Hegarty (captain), T. Wright
(president), I. Fraser, A. Renwick, G. H. Willison, R. G. Turnbull.

SIR CHAY BLYTH

Hawick's intrepid Transatlantic Rower and Global Yachtsman. In 1966, along with Captain John Ridgeway, he took just 90 days to row across the North Atlantic Ocean from Cape Cod, Massachusetts to the Aran Islands, Ireland. In 1971, he became the first person to sail single-handed and non-stop around the world in a westerly direction against the prevailing winds and currents.

BILLY HODGINS
Arguably one of the greatest 1950s middle distance runners that Hawick has ever produced. His professional world record time of 1min 53.6secs for the 880 yards on a grass track was recorded at Keswick in 1956 and still stands to this day.

WAYNE HOGG
The young Hawick jockey, who has been delivering high quality performances, is a great prospect for the future.

JIM RENWICK

The Hawick and Scotland centre three-quarter seen here speaking to Dr Dannie Craven,
Mr Rugby, during the 1980 British Lions tour of South Africa.

KEITH DALGLEISH

On board "Smart Predator" and racing to victory in the historic
SportingOdds.com Grey Horse Handicap at Newmarket.

CRAIG DOUGLAS

Described as one of Teviotdale Harriers greatest ever athletes, he had a most distinguished international track and cross-country running career.

TEVIOTDALE HARRIERS RELAY TEAM, 1910.

Winners of the Wyoming Silver Challenge Cup which was donated by Hawick Callants in the USA.

From left to right standing:
W. R. Sutherland, A. J. Grieve
From left to right seated:
J. S. Turnbull, R. H. Burton

WATTIE SUTHERLAND

W. R. Sutherland, the Scottish international winger and athlete who must surely rank as one of the all time greats.

A. J. GRIEVE

The first of Teviotdale Harriers' internationalists who ran for the Scottish cross country team in 1907.

J. S. TURNBULL

Member of the Teviotdale Harriers one mile relay team who won the Wyoming Silver Challenge Cup at the Hawick Common Riding games in 1910.

ROBERT H. BURTON

Teviotdale Harriers' only Olympic athlete who ran 800 metres race in Stockholm in the 1912 Olympics.

DAVID CAVERS
Teviotdale Harriers Scottish international athlete who has gained over 25 national vests in cross-country events. He has also represented Britain in the marathon and competed for Scotland in the 1998 Commonwealth Games.

HUGH F. McLEOD
The former Hawick, Scotland and British Lions prop who accumulated 40 international caps and played in two Lions tours.

LH
top

Photographs courtesy of Richard Allison.

JIMMIE GUTHRIE

Hawick's motorcycle racing legend who took part in his first TT at the Isle of Man in 1923.
He won his first TT Lightweight in 1930. From 1927 to 1937 he rode for Norton and AJS in
all key race meetings and became European Champion in 1935. He died tragically in 1937
following an accident in the German Grand Prix.

DARCY ANDERSON

Former Scottish internationalist winger who scored two tries against the mighty All Blacks on his debut appearance. Joining Huddersfield Rugby League team, he quickly became a firm favourite with the fans and spent seven years with the club.

TONY STANGER

No doubting the delight on the Hawick winger's face after scoring the winning try for Scotland in 1990 to clinch the Grand Slam victory over England in the championship decider at Murrayfield.

DAVE VALENTINE

Hawick's post-war rugby internationlist who went on to play rugby league for Huddersfield, winning 15 caps for Great Britain and captaining the national team in 1954.

DAVE McCOMBE

Seven times Borders Billiards Champion and three times winner of the Border Snooker Singles Championship.

RONNIE MURPHY
The 1950/60s Scottish front crawl champion over 50, 100 and 200 yards. He was also a Scottish waterpolo internationalist.

KENNY LAIDLAW
Hawick's Olympic cyclist seen here in one of the Tour de France race stages during the 1960s.

IRENE WILSON, JULIE FORREST, MARGARET STAVERT
The Scottish (1997) and British Isles Triples Champions (1998).

GRAHAM F. SMITH
Former Scottish Solo Trials Champion of the 1980s and winner of three British Sidecar Championship Trials.

JULIE FORREST

Hawick's talented Scottish internationalist bowler who was selected to represent Scotland at the 1998 Commonwealth Games in Kuala Lumpur.

INTERNATIONAL BOWLING HONOURS
Scottish Indoor Internationalist
From 1992

Scottish Indoor Pairs
1992, 1994, 2003/2004

Scottish Indoor Triples
1993

Scottish Indoor Singles
2001/2002, 2003/2004

Scottish Masters
2001/2002, 2002/2003, 2003/2004

British Isles Singles
2003/2004

World Indoor Mixed Pairs
2001/2002,2002/2003

World Indoor Singles
2003/2004

RUSSELL MOLLOY

Special Olympic European Games swimmer. He took part in the 50m breast stroke and back stroke events at Groningen, Holland, in the 2000 Games and has been involved for more than 15 years with Special Olympics.

157

JUDITH ANDERSON
Hawick's outstanding leading lady golfer has a string of titles to her credit. In a most remarkable career, she has won the ladies club championship on twelve separate occasions and the Border championship six times.

C. W. (SID) TELFER
Captain of Hawick Golf Club in 1952/53. He was club champion 14 times altogether.

STEVE HISLOP

The famous motorcycle racing ace with 11 TTs to his name was one of the greats of his generation. Tragically killed in a helicopter accident near Hawick in 2003.

Photo by kind permission of Derek Lunn.

T. F. (ERIC) GRIERSON

A great servant to cricket and rugby in Hawick, he played for Hawick & Wilton and "The Greens" before making his mark as a district umpire and international referee in these sports. He was also Scottish Cricket President in 1997.

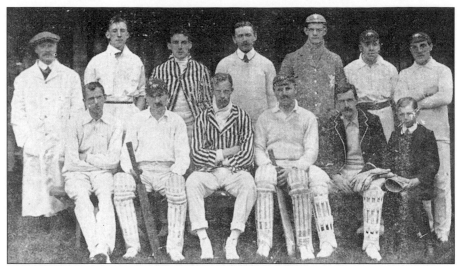

HAWICK & WILTON CRICKET TEAM, 1910

Back row (l to r): A. Hogg (umpire), J. D. Wilson, J. Storrie, R. Turnbull, F. D. Cairns,
Smith (prof.), T. Storrie
Front row (l to r): G. A. Blaikie, W. Storrie, I. G. Wallis (capt.), A. Turnbull, H. K. Oswald,
J. Hunter (scorer)
Hawick and Wilton Cricket Club, founded in 1849, is the oldest sports club in the town.

HAWICK & WILTON CRICKET TEAM

The 1st XI side of season 1959, who won the Border League title for the first time,
captained by Eric Grierson.

COLIN DEANS
The former Greens and Lions hooker who won 52 caps for Scotland to make him the joint record holder along with Jim Renwick and Tony Stanger.

GREENS WINNING SEVEN
The famous 1965/66 team who won all of the spring sevens tournaments and went on to record the famous ten-in-a-row run of victories.

COLIN COOK AND JAKE MCCOMBE

In the 1971 world championships held in Jacobsberg, Sweden, both archers captured world titles whilst representing Scotland. Colin (left) won the World Junior title whilst Jake beat all-comers to take the World Field Archery Championship crown.

THE FINNIE BROTHERS

Frank, Donald and Dave, the well known local boxers, who inspired many of Hawick's budding young talent on to greater heights. For many years after the war, Frank offered boxing lessons in the Stonefield Hall at Slitrig Crescent.

JOHN HAMILTON

Long serving member of the Teviotdale Harriers club both as an athlete and dedicated administrator, seen here with Alan Walker, a well known local athlete.

A team photograph of Hawick Ladies Hockey Club taken on the astroturf pitch at Tweedbank where the team played their home fixtures.
Back row (l to r): Rhona Suddon, Rose Wallace, Dianne Lauder, Ruth Hounam, Lisa Oliver, Fiona Turnbull, Carole Allott, Emma Dodd.
Front row (l to r): Anne Teague, Jackie Wilson, Tracey Sharp, Sheila Crowford, Ann Welsh

HAWICK ROYAL ALBERT FOOTBALL CLUB

Hawick Royal Albert F.C. with one of their first pieces of East of Scotland silverware in the 1960s.
Back: Thomson, Seath, Proudfoot, Brouch, McDonald, Doherty.
Front: Bagan, Nolan, McFarlane, Cleghorn, Anderson.

Hawick Royal Albert F.C. v Carlisle F.C. in the early 1980s. Seated fourth from right in the middle row, prior to transferring to Newcastle United then Liverpool, is Peter Beardsley who went on to win 58 England caps. Second from the right in the back row is Carlisle United's player manager, Bobby Moncur. The defender also played for Hearts and Newcastle United and gained 16 Scotland caps.

Hawick Industry

Compiled by
Raymond T Telfer
William Thomson
Gordon McDonald
Sam Barker

ENGINEERING TRADE

OVER THE PAST 100 years, engineering companies have provided a valuable support to industry within the town. The main contenders have been:

James Melrose & Sons Ltd. (General Engineering & Foundry)
Edward Walker (Textile Engineers)
George Woodcock & Sons Ltd. (Textile Engineers)
Turnbull & Scott Ltd. (General Engineers)
John Laurie Ltd. (Textile Engineers)
Mansfield Engineering Ltd. (General Engineers)
Ross Gordon Engineering Ltd. (General Engineers)

Ian Watson and Trevis Mabon working on a radial drill.

JAMES MELROSE & SONS LTD.

In today's world, engineering as a trade or a profession has an ever-decreasing status, but when the Hawick woollen trade was at its height it was the trade to be in, especially if one worked for Messrs. James Melrose & Sons who had a reputation in engineering and the training of apprentices that spanned the globe.

James Melrose was born in the Midlothian parish of Ratho in 1777 and was apprenticed as a millwright, eventually moving to Tweedmouth where he may have been employed by Mr George Black in his Tweedmouth boiler works, thus securing an insight into steam technology.

In Kelso on 11th November 1803, James Melrose married Helen Hardie, who came from the same family as Baillie John Hardie, and settled in Hawick around 1815, finding premises in Brougham Place, where he established Messrs. James Melrose & Sons.

From these early beginnings they were on the "cutting edge" of the new technology that was beginning to impact on the local woollen trade. In 1832 they installed a steam engine into Messrs. William Wilson & Sons, Ladylaw Mill, the first in Hawick. Mr D. Watson writing in Hawick Archaeological Transaction of 1868 noted their achievements:

> *"Various modes for producing an endless roving were tried, but none of them succeeded satisfactorily; and it was reserved for our townsman, Mr John Melrose, in 1844, at once to obviate the difficulty, and to enable carders to be used of any width, by the invention of the 'piecing machine'."*

So successful was this invention that it was adopted throughout Scotland and England, some were even sent to Russia.

James Melrose's two sons, John and Adam entered the firm, and after their father's death on the 10th September 1853 aged 76, they removed from Brougham Place to the "Whiskyhouse Mill" in Slitrig Crescent, which they retained till their demise in 1980.

In addition to their millwright business, they also produced threshing mills, steam engines and machinery for milling houses. In 1883 they designed and fitted out Eastfield Mills for Messrs. Blenkhorn, Richardson & Co., which is a striking example of their work.

James Melrose's grandson, John Melrose, CBE (1854–1927), was one of the original members of Hawick Callants Club and had the honour to serve as Hawick Provost from 1902–1919. During his tenure he was the first to wear the Provost's robes and chain donated by the Callants Club. After his retirement, the business was taken over by Joseph Price Laing, who had the distinction as serving as a fighter pilot in the First World War.

Messrs James Melrose & Sons had, over the years, developed a foundry business that produced manhole covers, gratings for drains and cast iron piping. Many parts produced in their foundry were machined and finished in their own workshops. They also supplied special castings to Messrs. George Woodcock & Sons for their textile machinery.

The retiral of "Joe" Laing in the late 1960's caused the business once again to change hands, Mr J. Brown, an employee, assumed the ownership.

Messrs. James Melrose & Sons, as millwrights and engineers, were closely linked to the local industry and when the mills began replacing their steam engines with electric motors, and the tweed industry in decline, their fortunes reflected this downturn in the market: the business. After some 165 years, Messrs James Melrose & Sons, Slitrig Crescent ceased trading in 1980. Throughout their long and distinguished business career, they provided a valuable contribution to the success of the Hawick woollen industry. They were the last firm in Hawick to produce their power from a waterwheel, which may have been installed in the 1770's.

The closure of Messrs. James Melrose & Sons led to the formation of two new companies'. Mansfield Engineering Ltd., which serves Hawick with general engineering, factory services, welding and boiler surveys. The other is Ross Gordon Engineering Ltd., which also provides the town with a general engineering service.

Jim Burgess, blacksmith at the forge.
This is an electric fan forge, replacing the manual bellows.

TURNBULL & SCOTT LTD., GENERAL ENGINEERS

Last year Turnbull & Scott celebrated its 70th year in business.

Originally incorporated in 1933 as Turnbull & Aitken, Engineers and Millwrights, the name was later changed to Turnbull, Aitken & Scott and eventually became Turnbull & Scott in 1955. Hunt Moscrop, a textile finishing machinery manufacturer based in Lancashire, acquired the company in 1969.

Since then it has been the subject of two management buyouts, the last one being in 1999 when the present directors, Mr C. Rowe and Mr J. Rafferty, bought the company in order to allow the managing director to retire.

During this period of evolution, the company has grown from its original concept of servicing textile mills in the Scottish Borders. General purpose work, fabrication, the manufacture of a finned tube and the acquisition of the Thermoiler unit heater has allowed the company to survive the decline of local manufacturing industries. It has now diversified into one of the largest engineering factories in the Borders region, sitting comfortably between the two coastlines.

Engineer Dave Scott with a replacement flywheel for Blenkhorn & Richardson, 1947, supplied by Turnbull & Scott.

Today the company designs, manufactures and installs products that not only serve the United Kingdom but the whole world and in the past few years has exported products to Lithuania, Germany, Russia, France and only recently exported special coils for sixteen large commercial greenhouses to the United States.

Currently the company is working on a project which will see 90 special unit heaters dispatched via Austria and Korea where they are ultimately destined for the Sakhalin Island (Russian) which is being developed as an offshore oil production unit for Japan.

Over the last four years the company has significantly invested in its people, training, machinery and property which stands it in good stead for continued development and expansion.

EDWARD WALKER, TEXTILE ENGINEER

Mr Walker was born in Nottingham and came to Hawick in 1893 when the company he was working for, Moses Mellor & Son, Hosiery Machine Builders, opened a business in the town. After a number of years Moses Mellor & Sons closed down in Hawick. Edward Walker decided to take over the assets of the business and started up his own company in 1909 at premises in Commercial Road, providing a repair and spare service to the knitwear industry in the town. His skills were quite considerable as can be seen from an old acceptance letter to his company from Peter Scott & Co. Ltd. dated 4th September 1916 confirming his quotation for altering their 6 division 30 Gauge machine to a 15 Gauge and re-erecting it for a cost of £166-15/- less two and a half percent.

GEORGE WOODCOCK & SONS LTD.

In 1928 Mr Walker sold his business to Mr George Woodcock, who in 1935 moved the business to larger premises in Commercial Road and formed the company, his twin sons Herbert and Sidney becoming directors. In 1943 the company became part of the Bentley Group, part of which was William Cotton Ltd., the renowned fully fashioned machine builders. During World War II they carried out sub-contract work for the Government, returning to textile engineering in 1945. Design and development became a major part of their business, producing a fast 12 section rib machine and many other attachments which could be retro fitted to machines. Among their many achievements was the tuck needle system for fully fashioned machines which was adopted by Wm. Cotton Ltd. and sold worldwide. These machines are still used within the Hawick knitwear industry today. Later developments included quilt and pillow roll packaging machines for the bedding industry.

Woodcock's (Monk Cotton International Ltd.) closed in 2003 due to a massive downturn in the textile market worldwide.

Woodcock's Machine Build Shop, 1985.
Left to right: Kenny Purvis, Wat Anderson, Jim White (Assembly Shop Foreman),
Ray Telfer (Managing Director), Allan Patterson (kneeling), Les Turnbull

Part of Woodcock's Machine Shop, 1985.

Woodcock's, Riversdale Mills, Mansfield Square, 1985.

173

Local technicians from various factories in the town being shown one of the first Bentley Cotton Mod 'B' fully fashioned machine installed in Hawick. Mr E. Start, Technical Director of Bentley Cotton, is explaining the machine. The photograph was taken in Braemar.
Some of those present included: Rob Crozier (Pringle), Jimmy Oliver (John Lauries), Bert Phaup (Turner & Rutherford), George Kerr (Turner & Rutherford), John Ferguson (Pesco), Bob Stark, Adam Balmer (Braemar), Gus Nixon (Lyle & Scott), Jim Crawford (Lyle & Scott), Bill Borthwick, Frank Simpson and Herbert Woodcock (all George Woodcock & Sons Ltd.)

JOHN C. LAURIE (HAWICK) LTD.

John Laurie served his apprenticeship with Robert Pringle & Sons Ltd. After World War II, he left the town for a short period of time to work in France. On his return he was employed by Peter Scott & Co. In 1946 he set up his own business in Beaconsfield Terrace in what is now the Jehovah's Witnesses Kingdom Hall. In 1954 he bought premises in Teviot Crescent where the company still carries out their business to this day.

WOOL TRADE

MESSRS MACTAGGART BROS., WOOL MERCHANTS

MESSRS MACTAGGART BROS., Wool Merchants, started in the early nineteen hundreds. Firstly as Messrs Elliot Mactaggart, then Mactaggart Brothers – R. L. Mactaggart and Ian C. Mactaggart (Cornet in 1928). Their skinworks were located in Albert Mills, Victoria Road, now occupied by Iceland supermarket. They also acquired premises in Buccleuch Street, St George's Lane, now the Royal Mail sorting office.

Dominion skins were imported from Australia and South Africa, which came by steamer to King George V Docks, Port Glasgow. These fleeces went to make woollen and worsted yarns.

Their premises at Wilton Mill, Commercial Road, handled fleece wool only, mainly from local farmers' annual wool clip, which was graded and sold at auction for the tweed and carpet trade. Messrs. Paton & Baldwin also purchased wool for the hand knitting market. Wool from "Blackface" sheep was exported to Italy for mattress manufacture. Shetland wool was also purchased, graded and sold mainly for the tweed industry, the finest being used for 9-gauge knitwear yarn. The pelts went to various tanneries for leather production.

J. Patterson, R. Edgar, W. Scott, J. Turnbull, R. Hunter, E. Casson, M. Halliday, W. Murphy

In the 1970s they discontinued to process skins and the company sold off Albert Mills, Wilton Mills and their works in Buccleuch Street and removed to new premises at Mansfield Road – sited beyond Hawick Rugby Football Ground – where they concentrated their business on handling wool.

Messrs Mactaggart Bros. was taken over by the Scottish Wool Growers and after a few years the business was removed to depots throughout the country. The Borders Regional Council purchased their large premises in Mansfield Road as a cleansing department.

At its peak of production Messrs Mactaggart Bros. employed approximately 80 to 90 personnel, including management and office staff.

Mactaggarts workers at Albert Mills, c.1950.

Back: Jock Edgar, Billy Scott, Matt Rowan, Jim Turnbull, Billy Hunter

Front: Eddie Casson, John Patterson, Robbie (Dyer) Edgar, Bob Hunter

Mactaggarts Skinworks, Hawick
"Bring 'em Back Alive" – Winners Fancy Dress Parade, c.1964
Back: Abe Nichol, Bill Murphy, Bill (Hare) Scott, Hughie Colville, Billy Cooper,
Jim Tulley, Bill (Voo) Robertson, Andrew Scott, Haig Cummings
Front: Drew Wilson, Rob Brunton, Jock Rae, Joe Brennan, Mick Halliday,
Jim (Pimpo) Anderson, Jock (Young Hare) Scott

Paddy Valentine,   *R. Edgar,*
Buccleuch Street, 1940.   *Buccleuch Street, 1940.*

THE HAWICK TWEED TRADE

Today the main industry in Hawick is the production of knitwear - high-class, fully-fashioned knitwear - but at the dawn of the 20th Century it was famed for the manufacture of Tweed. Scotch Tweed made in Hawick stood as a mark of quality throughout the world. An American journal in 1882 reminded its readers that Hawick, Scotland, was a town famous for the excellence of its Scotch tweeds.

In 1906, James Edgar, a founder of Hawick Callants Club, published his "Hawick Guide and Directory" which included a register of all the manufacturers engaged in the Hawick Tweed Trade:

Blenkhorn, Richardson & Co., Ltd., Eastfield Mills.
Dickson & Laings, Wilton Mills.
Dyson & Co. Ltd., Commercial Mills.
Greenwood, Watt, Howlands Mills.
Kedie & Darling & Co., Riversdale Mills.
Wm. Laidlaw & Sons, Teviot Crescent Mills.
Robert Noble & Co., Glebe Mills.
Alex. Paton & Co. Ltd., Albert Mills.
Scoon & Hood, Teviotdale Mills.
Sime, Williamson & Co., Weensland Mills.
Scott & Co., Trowmill.
Tait, Ballantyne & Co., Waverley Mills.
William Watson & Sons, Dangerfield Mills.
Wilson & Glenny Ltd., Langlands and Ladylaw Mills.

Weaving shed, Blenkhorn and Richardson.

From the collection at Hawick Museum

It was the advent of the 1815 Corn Laws, aggravated by the poor harvests of 1816-1817 and the subsequent loss of trade, which persuaded Messrs Wilson & Watson to introduce weaving into their hosiery business.

In 1832 Messrs William Watson & Sons, Dangerfield Mills, invoiced one of their London customers for a consignment of "tweel" which they misread, and re-ordered as "tweed". William Watson & Sons then decided to rename the weave from "tweel" to "tweed." This inspired decision was not only fortuitous for William Watson, but also for the Hawick woollen manufacturers, who, for the first time, had something to market: TWEED!

Scotch Tweed, Made in Hawick became synonymous with quality, a name that would launch the town on the international stage, a name that became part of the English language. At its zenith the tweed trade became the town's major employer. The wealth generated from the tweed trade can still be seen, reflected in the large imposing mansions erected by the tweed manufacturers: "Kilmeny", "Stirches", and "Hazelwood".

The Hawick tweed trade's main export market was North America, but the implementation of the 1890 American McKinley Act, which imposed swingeing tariffs on high class imported woollen goods, began to erode the fortunes of the tweed manufacturers. Such were the adverse trading

conditions that before the first decade of the 20th Century was over, two of the leading and longest established, manufacturers ceased trading; Messrs Dicksons & Laing's, (est. 1810) and Messrs Wm. Laidlaw & Sons, (est. 1811) There were no buyers!

The outbreak of the First World War gave the Hawick tweed trade a much-needed respite with the manufacturers producing "khaki" for the armed forces.

Burst flywheel, Blenkhorn and Richardson, 1947.

From the collections at Hawick Museum.

179

Wilson and Glenny's, 1959.

Courtesy of Hawick Camera Club.

Wilson and Glenny's, 1961, re-built after the fire.

From the collections at Hawick Museum.

During the hungry twenties and thirties, the Hawick tweed trade, along with the rest of the country, was severely restricted. However, the renewed armed conflict between 1939 and 1945 delivered, once again, a measure of stability and prosperity to the beleaguered trade.

The post-war boom years re-opened the lucrative but fickle American market. Mr James R. Scott-Noble, senior partner in Messrs Robert Noble, Glebe Mills, estimated that the value of overseas exports during 1956 was £4,848,000; £722,000 more than the first half of 1955, with the U.S.A. and Canada accounting for over 71 percent of their sales.

Despite this optimistic assessment, a malaise was slowly creeping through the industry. Home markets began to fall, and with the re-introduction of American trade tariffs in the late 1950s accompanied by fierce competition from continental Europe and the Far East, the Hawick tweed trade slid into decline.

It should be remembered that the tweed trade, unlike the knitwear trade, was a more complex and costly affair. The large tweed manufacturers controlled every stage of production from the purchase of raw wool through carding, spinning, weaving, to the final finishing process. This system, however, had its drawbacks. As manufacturers, they could not control, or have any influence over, the final garment. When tweed manufacturing was at its height this system proved effective but when the trade declined finances were not available to sustain it.

By the mid-1950s this approach to tweed manufacturing was still operating in the four large remaining manufacturers, Messrs Wilson & Glenny Ltd; Scoon & Hood & Co.; Blenkhorn, Richardson & Co Ltd; and Robert Noble & Co. Messrs William Watson & Sons, however, decided to abandon weaving and concentrate their business on yarn spinning for the resurgent knitwear industry.

Britain may well have experienced the freedom of the swinging sixties, but that same decade witnessed the collapse of the Hawick tweed trade. The traditional markets were in decline; fashions had changed, in some cases, beyond imagination at that time. The tweed producing firm's future prospects looked less certain. To counter this downturn in the market, several of the businesses amalgamated into larger groupings, but despite Herculean efforts, one by one they ceased trading.

By the end of the 1970s, the era of large tweed mills was almost over. Of James Edgar's original list of manufacturers engaged in the Hawick tweed trade only one large manufacturing unit remained, Messrs Wilson & Glenny Ltd. All, however, was not lost. Trowmill, now renamed Wrights of

Trowmill Ltd., continued to weave and a new weaving company Teviotex Ltd. was established.

To extend their traditional markets, Wrights of Trowmill Ltd. departed from past restrictions by establishing a retail outlet, selling a range of local knitwear to complement their cloth.

This was an industry convinced that it produced the finest range of cloth; an industry that was proud of its traditions and skills; an industry whose reputation for quality was second to none in the market places of the world. In 2004 Messrs Wrights of Trowmill Ltd., and Teviotex Ltd., are the only two remaining manufacturers of a product in which Hawick's dominance was globally recognised.

The golden era of Hawick tweed is one that may well be over. Nevertheless, its illustrious and distinguished record cannot be denied. It stands as a testimony to the vision of its early pioneers and the enterprise of its subsequent entrepreneurs. It is a piece of our history in which we should rightly take pride.

It is hoped that this exhibition will rekindle interest in the once much acclaimed Hawick Tweed Trade, a trade that brought wealth, prosperity and international recognition to our town.

Trow Mill Shop, 2003.

Warpers and Power Looms

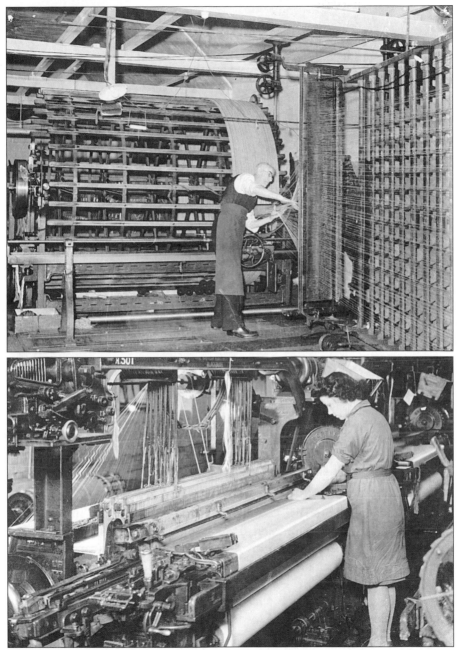

From the collections at Hawick Museum.

Dyeing and Finishing

Circa 1929

MESSRS JOHN TURNBULL & SONS, DYERS & FINISHERS

MESSRS JOHN TURNBULL & SONS, founded in Hawick in 1819, was the oldest surviving commission dyehouse in the Scottish Borders. The founder's grandfather was also involved in a carpet factory and when that business failed, he ran a dyehouse in Hawick from the late 1700s until the early 1800s. Although few early records are in existence, it is known that much of the business carried out was the dyeing of wool for the thriving spinning industry in the town. As was common the colouring materials used were logwood, indigo, cochineal, etc. Much of the indigo dyed wool was used in the manufacture of the blue and white striped butcher aprons.

Around 1880 the firm started to undertake the dyeing of domestic garments for the general public, mainly 'blacks' for mournings. This being subsequently developed into more general dyeing and cleaning with the introduction of the new French (Dry) Cleaning using benzine in the 1890's. Agencies to collect garments were established in various towns in Scotland and north east England as far south as Hull.

In 1898, John Turnbull & Sons purchased the business of A. Butler & Co., who ran a commission dyehouse at Wauchope Mills in Langholm. However, the company declined the renewal of the lease in the early 1900s because of the poor state of trade!

With the lease of their premises in Teviot Road due to expire in 1913, a site was obtained in Slitrig Crescent where a new dyeworks was erected.

In 1900 John Turnbull & Sons became part of the British Cotton and Wool Dyers Association, although continuing to trade under its own name. An inventory dated 1909 shows plant including an oval paddle for garment dyeing, numerous wooden vats and lead lined brick boiling cisterns, steam driven hydro-extractors by Broadbent, and mainly gas lighting.

In common with most other Border Commission dyehouses John Turnbull & Sons continued to provide facilities for loose stock, yarn and piece dyeing for the local manufacturers, although having a strong

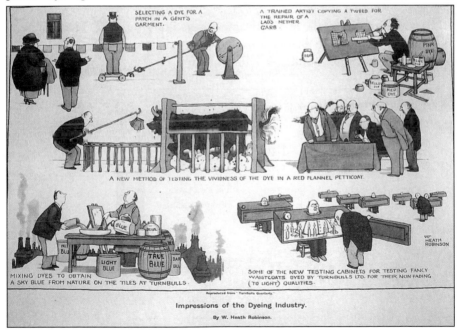

Impressions of the Dyeing Industry by W. Heath Robinson

specialisation in the dyeing of indigo, having no less than 14 indigo vats in 1918. Woven cloth scouring, milling and finishing was also part of the service offered, as was raw wool sorting scouring and drying.

Throughout the 1920s and 1930s the changes which took place were few. The replacement of wooden machines with stainless steel; improved dyestuffs and dyeing techniques; the closure of Cochrane Smith & Co., Selkirk in 1930 with the transfer of 4 Klauder Weldon machines to Slitrig Crescent. Package dyeing replaced hank dyeing in the 1940's, being finally discontinued in 1970.

About 1911 a site was acquired in Victoria Road, and a factory erected to accommodate the now substantial domestic garment dyeing and dry cleaning activities. A separate company was formed trading as Turnbull's Ltd., which commenced operations in 1914 in a new custom built factory at Howlands to carry out the domestic dyeing and dry and wet cleaning operations formerly being done by John Turnbull & Sons.

Modern, open plan, mainly single storey buildings provided excellent facilities for employees along with adequate water supplies from their own well. Throughout the 1920s & 1930s considerable expansion of business took place by means of a strong marketing advertising policy with the company's name becoming well-known through out the British Isles and overseas.

By this time the bulk of the business was done by post. The company successfully applied to the Postmaster to obtain the first pre-paid postal packet licence whose number was P.P.1, below.

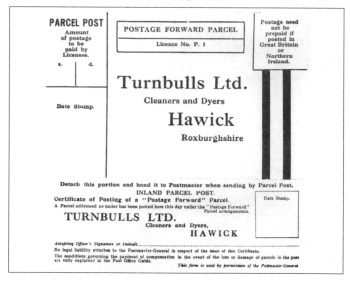

186

Diversification into the dyeing and finishing of stockings for the local industry also took place in the 20s with the shrink resist treatment and bleaching of underwear following soon after. These developments requiring further extension of the premises in 1917, 1919 and 1922.

The dyeing and finishing of knitted outerwear followed in the late 20s along with dyeing and finishing of woven and knitted woollen fabrics, also sulphur bleaching of hand knitting yarns. Over a ton per day of single jersey fabric was being dyed and cloth-finished by the early 1940s. Further building extensions, including a new piece-dyehouse and boiler house, were completed in 1937.

In 1937, the Dri-sol shrink resist process was introduced and developed during the period 1939-45. Considerable quantities of socks were treated by the Warnorm process. The Lan-fix shrink resist process, patented by J. L. Sharp in 1947, for which he was made a Fellow of the Textile Institute, was developed commercially at Turnbulls Ltd.

The introduction of acrylic fibres in the 1950s saw the company extending into this field and seeking new markets in the Midlands and London. They were among the first to apply flat finishing techniques to Courtelle fabrics in the late 1950s and early 60s.

By the late 1950s increasing postal charges and the growth of unit cleaners had seriously eroded the dry cleaning and dyeing business. A chain of receiving shops in Edinburgh & Glasgow proved unsuccessful, and so in 1965 the domestic garment-dyeing department was closed and the cleaning interests sold off to other companies.

In 1966/7 high temperature winches were installed to handle polyester dyeing and a further extension was built to house two heat setting stenters. Jet dyeing machinery followed in the early and mid 70s. The company, by this time concentrating mainly on knitted fabrics including cotton stretch terry fabrics, employed a labour force of about 100 operating on 3 shifts. The output of about 35 tonnes per week was transported by the firm's own fleet of vans to Lancashire, Yorkshire, the Midlands and London. However, escalating transport costs, problems of distance and a decline in the volume of polyester led to the closure of the plant in 1980.

Rationalisation by the British Cotton and Wool Dyers Association in the 1970s combined both Victoria Road and Slitrig Crescent works under the trading title of Turnbull Dyers (Hawick) Ltd., later to be changed to Cawdaw Dyers Ltd., trading as Turnbull the Dyers.

With the closure of the Victoria Road works in 1980, the knitted cotton dyeing section was transferred to Slitrig Crescent. The premises were extended during the period 1935 to 1956 and following a fire in 1959 a KD permanent setting machine was installed. With the collapse of the parent group Cawdaw Industrial Holdings in February 1982, the company went in to receivership but continued to operate the works in its entirety under the existing management. Then in January 1983 a new company formed by four members of the management, trading under the original name of John Turnbull & Sons, acquired the premises and plant from the receiver and re-commenced dyeing and finishing operations. In October 1996 the company took over the Galashiels based dyeing and finishing business of Gladstone's KB, integrating both businesses at Slitrig Crescent.

December 1998 saw McNaughton Holdings Ltd. of Pitlochry, one of their principal customers, acquiring a majority holding in the company. The business still continued to operate as a commission processor, but to an ever-diminishing number of textile manufacturers within the Borders and throughout the U.K. Finally the company decided to call in the receivers in February 2002, thus ending some 183 years of dyeing and finishing in Hawick.

Start of the demolition of the main chimney, Slitrig Crescent, July 1983.

From the collections at Hawick Museum.

HAWICK HOSIERY TRADE

THE HOSIERY TRADE was originally of the "custom" kind, stockings being made on a machine introduced by Bailie John Hardie in 1771. It was not until the year 1780 that a hosier, Mr John Nixon, began to make goods for the general market from his twelve stocking frames. Business from across the Border flourished up until the Napoleonic Wars. Subsequent development by the early pioneers such as William Wilson, William Watson, William Beck and Dicksons & Laings firmly established the hosiery trade as the main industry in the town. Carpet making, incle weaving and spinning had fallen by the wayside.

In 1794 the future of the industry was to be changed forever. William Beck did engage to teach John Pringle the trade of stocking making and, in the course of time, he was to have the biggest influence on the hosiery industry in Hawick of all time, becoming the founder in 1815 along with brother Robert of what is now "Pringle of Scotland".

It has to be remembered that the early manufacturers always described themselves as woollen manufacturers, with several firms producing both hosiery and tweeds. During the 1860s, several of the woollen manufacturers decided to abandon hosiery and concentrate their efforts on the more lucrative tweed trade.

Peter Adamson, founder of Adamson and Scott, in the early 1900s in his "stocking shop",
Drumlanrig Place.

James Bonsor Boarding House, c.1910.

From the collections at Hawick Museum.

James Bonsor Milling House, c.1910.

From the collections at Hawick Museum.

James Bonsor Knitting Flat, c.1910.

From the collections at Hawick Museum.

The early years of the 20th century saw the end of the pioneering days and several new young manufacturers who came from humble beginnings were beginning to make their impact on the market place: Peter Scott, William Lockie, Messrs Lyle & Scott and Messrs Turner & Rutherford.

William Cotton of Loughborough invented his Patent Frame in 1864 and sometime between 1850 and 1858 Cotton's Patent-knitting frame was eventually accepted and introduced into Messrs John Laing's, Slitrig Crescent. This brought about the demise of the old stocking frame, sometimes referred to as "the four posts of misery". Once established, this "Hi-Tech" machine eventually brought the long yearned prosperity to the hosiery trade. Modified types of Cottons Patent Frames still form the bulk of plain knitting in the industry today.

An examination of the early manufacturers' sales catalogues gives an indication of their qualities and the varieties of the yarn employed. They also show the huge range of underwear for sale. Long Johns for the gentlemen, knitted underwear for the children and several fetching fashion items for the ladies' range.

The First World War interrupted their progress when they were required to produce garments for the government. With the end of hostilities, the difficult inter-war years reduced their production. The world and fashions

Hendersons Boarding House, 1911.

From the collections at Hawick Museum.

changed to accommodate the new expectations of the population. Knitted underwear was losing its appeal due to the advent of central heating. The Hawick manufacturers were aware of this shift in the market place, and began to introduce knitted outerwear. Such was their faith in the new fashion trend of the future that Messrs Peter Scott – Pesco's – decided to erect a new factory before the war.

Lyle & Scott's seaming department.

From the collections at Hawick Museum.

Pringle's fire, 1939.

From the collections at Hawick Museum.

Woollen outerwear became popular with women round about 1920 and in 1930 fashion changed to body hugging designs. One of the early leaders was Innes, Henderson (Braemar Knitwear Ltd.) whose goods were in great demand.

Innes, Henderson was reluctant to give up their underwear trade and in

Towerknowe and Elliots' Mill behind.

From the collections at Hawick Museum.

the late 1920s were prepared to break with tradition and introduce cut and sew. They purchased the small firm of A. Brodie & Co. which made "Kumfy" products, but with customer complaints regarding their double quality standard, it was never a success and consequently lost their status as "pace setter" to Pringle. The Great Depression of 1929 did not help the situation.

The years following the Second World War saw the hosiery trade develop into the present day industry, when the balance between underwear and knitted outerwear began to favour the outerwear market. They then came to use the term "knitwear"; but those of a certain vintage always referred to the trade as the "hosiery". Old habits die hard. However, in 1936 Messrs Lyle and Scott appointed a Viennese designer, named Dr Hamor, and along with Mr C. D. Oliver in 1938 introduced a revolutionary new type of underwear garment under licence from Cooper's, America, the famous "Y-Front". This cut and sew fabric was knitted on circular knitting machines

Sheep shearing, the first stage in "Pesco" manufacturing.

From the collections at Hawick Museum.

Peter Scott's, Buccleuch Street, c.1924.

From the collections at Hawick Museum.

New barfillers flat, Braemar, 1960.
Courtesy of Hawick Camera Club.

Braemar, 1960.
Courtesy of Hawick Camera Club.

and developed into a highly lucrative business until it was removed from Hawick in 1960 and transported to Gateshead and Dunfermline.

Pringle's success was probably due to a young designer from Vienna who had trained under Bernhard Altmann, by the name of Otto Weisz, who was appointed in 1934 and was soon to establish his own authority and the name of Pringle on the world stage of knitwear designs, which were known as "dressmaker styles."

The greatest development that firmly established Hawick as the main centre of knitwear was the introduction of the "Twin-Set" and some of the far-sighted manufacturers employed several world famous international designers; Christian Dior, Gina Fratina, etc. A Hawick Twin-Set made in cashmere or lambswool was soon to be worn by the famous film stars of the

Walter Wilson's.
Courtesy of Hawick Camera Club.

Clean binding to attach collars to garments, Pringle's Mill.

day. Pringle & Co. signed up international sportsmen such as Arnold Palmer and Gary Player. The rich and fashionable of the international set wore the highly expensive, hand-made cashmere intarsia garments. These were the golden days of the trade when Hawick knitwear virtually sold itself.

Following the end of hostilities in 1945, the knitwear industry began to take off, gradually moving towards full time manufacture of outerwear garments. Companies began to install new and faster knitting machines (frames) to cope with the demand.

Geordie Middlemas, hand knitter (front), Pringle's Mill.

Knitting frames in the extension at Johnston's of Elgin.

Supplied by Johnston's of Elgin.

Intarsia frame at Johnston's of Elgin.

Supplied by Johnston's of Elgin.

Styling also played an important part with the use of "Striping – Lace/Cable and Tuck stitch machines".

However, at the zenith of their international repute, they fell victim in the 1960s and 1970s to the avarice of outside entrepreneurs, who gradually made their presence felt in the local industry. Long established family businesses such as Messrs Innes Henderson (Braemar) were bought out by Mr Hugh Fraser. Pringle's was taken over by the Dawson Group and Lyle & Scott found themselves included into the Wolsey Group. For the first time, individuals unknown in the town were taking decisions that effected the Hawick companies and their workforce in boardrooms far removed from Hawick.

In 1970/71 short time working befell the knitwear industry in Hawick and continued until late 1972 before full time working was resumed.

The Hawick manufacturers were always fully aware of the new technical developments that were coming onto the market place. The classic fully fashioned knitted garments were in the main knitted on Cottons Patent Model "A", and the much loved Model "B", eventually the Model "E" was introduced, and the "Monks Samco-matic" found its way into several factories.

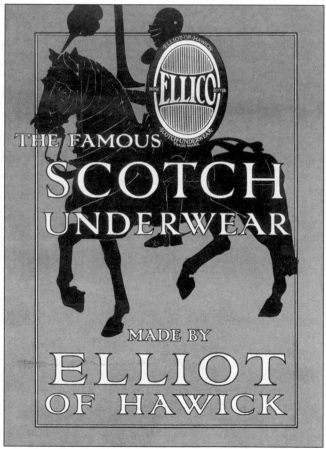

The 1980s saw the introduction of the electronic Vee-bed knitting machine developed by a Japanese company, "Shima Seiki," which opened new design possibilities for the manufacturers. They also introduced an entirely new concept of technical brilliance the "Complete Garment Knitting Machine" that did just what it says; it knits complete garments. The machine also has extra facilities that brings the Hawick Hosiery Trade back full circle; it knits stockings!

Over the past one hundred years the Hawick hosiery trade has witnessed many changes, some not always to its advantage, the take-over fever of the past has left the industry the poorer and seen the industry shrink to a shadow of its former self. Several manufacturers have disappeared, others have been amalgamated into larger holdings resulting in their famous trade names being discarded.

Overseas production has greatly under-cut the foundations of the industry; nonetheless the present manufacturers have been able to develop their own high-class niche market. The introductions of scarves, gloves, stockings and various accessories compliment the traditional classic fully-fashioned garment trade and it is hoped that these new trends will keep Hawick in the forefront of these ever changing and challenging times.

Throughout its distinguished history the Hawick knitwear trade has always striven to produce an honest, high-class garment of quality and

Pringle scouring house. Frank Halliday is on the right.

199

design, a garment that still continues to find its place in the international market.

The past twenty five years has seen new companies join the long established list of successful knitwear manufacturers in Hawick: namely, Johnston's of Elgin, Barker of Scotland, N. Peal Cashmere Ltd., Hawick Cashmere Co. Ltd., Douglas of Scotland Ltd., Shorts of Hawick. etc.

From small beginnings these companies are now world renowned and at the top of the Scottish cashmere business and collectively employ over 550 staff, each having their own retail outlets throughout the U.K. and around the world.

A new period in the history of Pringle of Scotland began appropriately at the beginning of a new millennium when the company was bought by S. C. Fang of Hong Kong, in March 2000.

Enormous changes have taken place within the industry throughout its history and the last few years have been no exception. The future of the industry in Hawick is once again reliant on the individual vision of its leaders to ensure that there will always be a place at the top for Hawick knitwear in the twenty first century.

We trust this exhibition will not only recall the memories of past glory days, but also illustrate the new developments that will continue to keep Hawick in the forefront of the knitwear trade.

Weensland Spinning Company and Heronhill greenhouses.
From the collections at Hawick Museum.

Weensland Spinning Mills

When James Edgar published his 1906 Guide and Directory of Hawick, he noted two spinning manufacturers, Weensland Spinning Company and Messrs. William Laidlaw & Sons, Teviot Crescent.

The origins of a spinning industry in Hawick can be traced back to 1780 when John Nixon, who, with several partners, established a small hosiery and spinning mill in the High Street. This partnership dissolved around 1795 when Messrs. John Nixon & Sons was formed, along with his sons Joseph and William Nixon, who became Hawick Cornet in 1813, erected a spinning mill at Lynwood in 1804. The business was sold in 1864 to, Messrs. Wm. Laidlaw, Tweed Manufacturer, Teviot Crescent Mills who eventually ceased trading in 1909, which left only one dedicated spinning mill in the town, Weensland Spinning Mill. The large tweed manufacturers processed and spun their own yarn.

The Weensland Spinning Company had its origins in 1830 when John Wilson, son of Wm. Wilson, Ladylaw Mills, decided to manufacturer flannel cloth from cheviot wool and in 1835 purchased Weensland Corn Mill.

John Wilson had a modern outlook towards his business. Transport from Hawick was laid on for the workers with a free cup of coffee, provided they arrived before the starting time of 6.05a.m. Houses were built near the mill at Weensland Terrace, a library and reading room was also made available. After the death of his father, Wm. Wilson in 1832, the three brothers, Walter, John and George decided in 1851 to divide the family business between them.

George Wilson, the first Provost of Hawick 1861–1868, gained Weensland Mills. He then assumed a partner, Mr Walter Armstrong Suddenly in May 1875, Messrs. Wilson & Armstrong, Tweed Manufacturers, collapsed with debts of £50,000, due to Mr Armstrong's unauthorised speculation on the London Stock Exchange. The business was then sold at auction for £36,000 to a Mr Charles Alexander, an Edinburgh merchant, who also purchased George Wilson's Heronhill Estate, including the mansion for £12,000 and the workers houses at Weensland Terrace for £2000, which he renamed Alexander Terrace. This business did not succeed and the company failed in 1884 with a British Linen Bank overdraft of some £70,000.

Around 1886 the Bank, who failed to find a buyer for Weensland Mills, then approached Messrs. Wilson & Glenny & Co. who eventually purchased the company for £7500, and decided to concentrate solely on the manufacture of woollen yarns; thus Weensland Spinning Company was established. The weaving sheds and looms were sold in 1889 to Messrs. Sime, Williamson & Co.

The dyeing and spinning of woollen yarn is a highly technical business, employing the services of an experienced staff with a fully equipped laboratory in order to produce the range of colours and qualities the woollen industry requires.

Such was the reputation of Weensland Spinning Company that the Textile Congress, held in Hawick in 1991, acknowledged they were "unrivalled in the production of expert handling of pure cashmere yarns and enjoyed a great reputation for the production of fancy Cheviot and Saxony yarns used in Scotch Tweeds and gave special attention to the production of coloured mixtures and twist yarns."

Over the years the fortunes of Weensland Spinning Company mirrored the fluctuations in the woollen trade that affected the rest of the town. During the difficult inter-war years, trading conditions saw a contraction in their business and, after the Second World War, those of a certain vintage may remember that Pringles of Scotland had a frame flat at the rear of their premises.

Weensland Spinning Company was not immune to the outside pressure and was eventually taken over by the large Bradford based Illingworth Morris Group. This same group owned the Hawick Cashmere Company.

The company was then sold to Courtaulds Textiles about 1980. Although they brought new investment to the firm, it was to no avail. The downturn in the textile market caused their parent company to end production in the early 1990's. It was ironic as Weensland Spinning Company closed its doors, the local knitwear manufacturers were not only importing yarn from Italy, but China! Thus, after a distinguished manufacturing record spanning some 104 years, Hawick had lost its only remaining dedicated spinning mill.

The former offices of Weensland Spinning Company have now been converted into the Tregus Weensland Function Suite. The main building was destroyed by fire.

Fashion House of Messrs. W. & O. Marcus Limited

TWO BROTHERS, namely Walter and Otto Marcus, originally from Westphalia in Germany, founded Messrs. W. & O. Marcus Ltd. In 1940 they established a Branch Factory of their London Fashion House, manufacturing ladies' high-class suits and dresses in Willglen Mill, 22 Commercial Road, Hawick, formally part of Messrs. Wilson & Glenny Ltd.

The Marcus brothers already knew of Hawick, its great tradition and the quality the workers brought to the industry through a close friend, Mr Otto Weisz, Head Designer with Pringles of Scotland.

One other reason for coming to Hawick was that the Londoners were having such a traumatic time during the blitz and having a Branch Factory gave Mr Walter Marcus the opportunity to send several of his workers to Hawick on a "working holiday". In 1942 there were still Londoners working in Hawick.

Mr Otto Marcus, the younger brother, stayed in London while Mr Walter Marcus settled in Hawick with his wife Anne and daughter Helen in Wellogate Villa until the mid 1950s when, owing to his brother's illness, he had to return to London.

Mr Walter Marcus was a very strict, generous employer, expected faithfulness, reliability, honesty and good workmanship. During the war time the apprentices were well looked after, starting half-an-hour later in the morning and every day getting one-third of a pint of milk or hot chocolate. The adults worked from 8.00am till 6.00p.m., with 1 hour for lunch and a ten minute break in the morning and afternoon and Saturdays from 8.00am till 11.00am with a ten minute break. At one time W. & O. Marcus Ltd. employed some 170–180 workers.

The Manageress was Mrs Frederica Rosenberger, Mrs R. as she was always referred to, was Hungarian, born in Budapest, a brilliant dressmaker and needlewoman. She was also a strict disciplinarian – there were no half measures – "Practice makes Perfect". All the work had to be perfect.

Mrs Ditta Kerpen, their London based head designer, Czechoslovakian by birth, along with Mrs Rosenberger and the Marcus's had to flee continental Europe during the 1930s due to the Hitler regimes oppressive policy towards the Jews.

Mr Otto Weisz started a blouse department in the mid 1940s and the "Pringle" girls came across to "Marcus's" to make the samples to Mrs Rosenberger's instructions.

During the years when Mr Walter Marcus lived in Hawick he arranged regular fashion shows in the Tower Hotel, now Drumlanrig's Tower, and brought the new samples, model girls, designers and managers up from London.

Most of the samples for the London Fashion House's spring, summer, autumn and winter collections were made in Hawick. Some of the materials used were exclusive, gorgeous to look at and feel, but not always easy to work. Silks from Switzerland, velvet, taffeta, grosgrain, watersilk, wool crepe, moss crepe, jersey jacquard fabric. Rawnsley & Brown Brothers also supplied elegant materials. Border Tweed and Wool Crepe came from Messrs. Gardiners of Selkirk and McNairn's, Corbie Lynn Mills, Selkirk.

W. & O. Marcus Ltd. used several brand names, Marcus, Marcusa, Jersey de Lux, and it was a tribute to the skill of the Hawick workers that these high-class designed and finished garments were ordered by some of the most prestigious fashion houses; Harrod's, Liberty's, Fortnum & Mason, Debenhams, Selfridges, Jenners, Bourne & Hollingsworth, Greensmith Downes, etc.

In those days Hawick railway station was a busy place, most of the Hawick factories receiving and despatching goods by rail. Every item needed for the manufacturing of the garments from pattern paper, to sewing thread, came from London by British Rail.

In the 1940s, Marcus's started sending their garments to London by rail each evening in boxes, packed carefully with tissue paper. This was expensive, as each garment had to be re-pressed in London the next day. After fibre trunks were introduced, they were able to pack each dress on a hanger and hang them on a rail fitted into the trunks. At 5.00pm each night, the railway van uplifed the trunks containing around 60–70 garments to be put on the 11.00pm "Pullman". Unfortunately the rail charges increased to a position where it became uneconomical and from Marcus's point of view, this was the "end of the line".

On Friday 30th October 1964, Messrs. W. &. O. Marcus Ltd., Willglen Mill, 22 Commercial Road, finally closed its doors for the last time after 24 years of manufacturing ladies high-class suits and dresses in Hawick.

Photograph of Messrs. W. & O. Marcus staff taken in London, c.1950.
Back left to right: Mr Otto Marcus, Mrs Anne Marcus (Walter's wife),
Mrs Alvine Marcus (Otto's wife), Mr Walter Marcus
Front row: Miss Helen Hill, Mrs Ditta Kerpen, Miss Ella Russell,
Mrs F. Rosenberger, Mrs Tista Tierney

The Callants Club
The First One Hundred Years

Presidents 1904 –1913 (from left to right)
Back row: Ex-Cornet W. T. Grieve, 1907, Ex-Cornet A. H. Drummond, 1906
Bailie Dechan, 1905, Tom Ker, 1904, Ex-Cornet J. E. D. Murray, 1909
Front row: Dr. W. T. Barrie, 1910, Provost Melrose, 1912, Bailie Lawson, 1913
J. G. Winning, 1911, A. R. Oliver, 1908

1903	8th December. First meeting
1904	19th February. First Annual Dinner when the principal guest was Tom Scott RSA.
	13th May. First Annual Congratulatory Smoker for the Cornet.
1906	The Callants' Club set up a committee to organise a public subscription for the purchase of a gold chain and robe of office for the Provost. On 14 September at a well attended function in the Town Hall the presentation was made by the President of the Club, A.H. Drummond to Provost John Melrose.
1914	At the end of the first decade of the Club and to coincide with the 400th Anniversary of the capture of the colour in 1514, the Club organised a Home Coming and Pageant during which overseas visitors were entertained and at the end of which the 1514 Memorial was unveiled.

Provost Melrose.

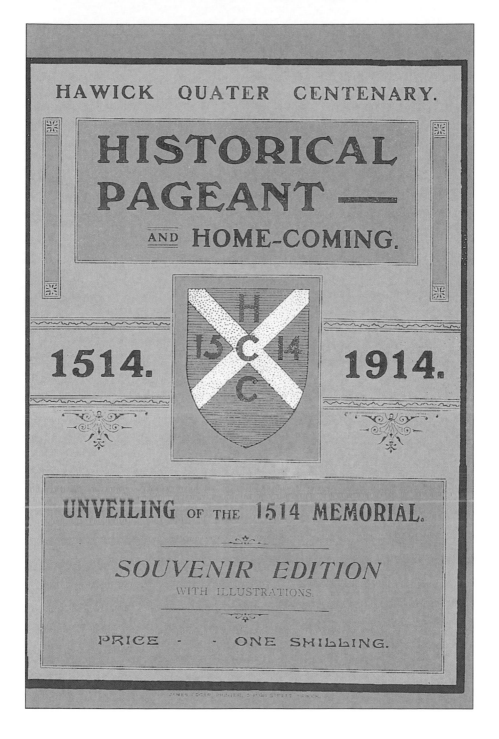

HAWICK QUATER CENTENARY.

HISTORICAL PAGEANT — AND HOME-COMING.

1514. **1914.**

UNVEILING OF THE 1514 MEMORIAL.

SOUVENIR EDITION

WITH ILLUSTRATIONS.

PRICE - - ONE SHILLING.

JAMES EDGAR, PRINTER, 5 HIGH STREET, HAWICK.

EPISODE IV.—THE CALL TO ARMS

EPISODE I.—TABLEAU.

OVERSEAS VISITORS AND MEMBERS OF HAWICK CALLANTS' CLUB AT DODBURN.

1916	On 12th July 1916 the Club marked the anniversary of the Gallopoli campaign by laying a wreath at the 1514 Memorial. The years passed without another mark of commemoration until 1930 since when the Club has paid annual tribute each 12th of July at the 1514 Memorial and the War Memorial.
1958	The Cornet, Right and Left Hand Men and Acting Father, together with all Standard Bearers etc and Provosts attending the Colour Bussing were formally invited to attend a Smoker after the Colour Bussing. This function is an annual event.
1964	Bouquets presented to local Hospitals and Old Folks Homes at the Common Riding and it was unanimously agreed that this should be done every year. New set of Provost's robes presented by the Club.
1965	Club marked 50th Anniversary of Gallipoli Campaign by sponsoring a Gallipoli Fund to enable some of the veterans of the 1/4th KOSB Gallipoli Comrades Association to take part in the 50th Anniversary pilgrimage to the Battle Fields.
1975	President attended Remembrance Day Service on Sunday 9th November and laid a wreath at War Memorial on behalf of the Club. This was the first time that the club had attended and it was agreed that this should become an annual event.

1976	Kings Own Scottish Borderers presented the Club with plaque as mark of gratitude of the Regiment in looking after the interests of the few remaining members of the Gallipoli Comrades Association.
1976	Proposals for the Composition of Future Common Riding Ceremonial and Administrative Committees prepared by the Club were approved and adopted by a public meeting of townspeople in November, bringing to a satisfactory conclusion the work of the Council and other organisations in this most important matter.
1979	On 6th May, The President presented the Honorary Provost with the new Provost's Chain which the Club had been instrumental in obtaining following the loss of the Chain presented to the former Town Council in 1906. This once again emphasised the part played by the Callants Club in preserving the traditions of the Town.
1984	Three inscribed flutes presented to the Drum and Fife Band.
1999	The Club formed a sub-committee to consider the restructuring of the Common Riding Committee. This sub-committee met with all other Common Riding Organisations of the town and made substantial progress.
2000	The Hawick Callants Club David Ferguson Memorial Trust was formed. The trust presents prizes annually at Hawick High School for Geography and also for a Special Achievement Award.
2002	The Club sponsored a competition for Common Riding Shop Window displays. Now an annual competition.

LITERATURE, ARTS, EDUCATION, etc.

1909	The first School Competition organised by the Club took place. In the early days they took the form of examination papers based on Robert Wilson's "History of Hawick" and Adam Laing's "Branxholm and the Land of the Scott's".
1922	The Club introduced a competitive examination in Local History and Folk Lore.

1927	The Club supported the publication of R S Craig's "Hawick and the Border" and James Turnbull's "Hawick in Bygone Days"
1931	The Club subsidised the publication of a new edition of "Hawick Songs"
1954	The book "The First Fifty Years of Hawick Callants Club" was published.
1957	The Club published a new Hawick Song Book.
1959	An essay competition at the Primary Schools and the High School was instituted and book tokens were given as prizes. This competition continues annually at all Primary Schools in the town.
1964	The first LP record of Hawick Songs was made.
1965	The second LP record of Hawick Songs was made.
1971	Old Common Riding films were transferred on to 16mm film and film of Common Ridings between 1929 and 1934 shown to members and friends.
1978	A new edition of "Hawick in Song and Poetry" was published.
1983	The Learning Project on the Common Riding and its Traditions by Ron Taylor was subsidised by the Club and 200 copies were made available to the Primary Schools for use in the Essay Competition.
1989	"Hawick in Song and Poetry" reprinted.
1991	Club contributed towards the publication of "The Place Names of Roxburghshire" by Mrs. Jessie Macdonald and "Lest We Forget" by Mrs Marjory Coltman.
1992	The Club negotiated with the National Film Archive for the transfer on to video of many old films of Hawick and Common Ridings. These have had public showings. The Club contributed towards a booklet published by the Archaeological Society on Adam Inglis' notes on Hawick songs. The Club donated to and offered assistance to the Will H. Ogilvie Fund which was formed to perpetuate and commemorate the name of this prominent Borders poet.

1998	A new updated edition of the Common Riding information folder which describes each part of the Common-Riding on a separate loose leaf page and is aimed principally at Primary Schools was published.
2001	The Club's two LPs of Hawick Songs were successfully transferred on to one CD. A considerably revised and updated "Hawick in Song and Poetry" dedicated to the late Frank Scott in recognition of his contribution to Hawick and it's traditions was published. A revised version of "Hawick Songs" with many more songs was published.
2002	The Club internet web site was set up.

MONUMENTS, MEMORIALS AND THE LIKE

The Club has been wholly responsible for, or has supported and contributed to, a considerable variety of monuments, memorials and the like of which the following is representative:

1905	George Fraser Macnee Memorial Fountain in Wilton Lodge Park
1910	The Club arranged to have The Moat restored and in 1911 the Club organised the erection of the Ca Knowe Memorial. Provost Melrose presided and the Cornet Will Thorburn was present at the unveiling.
1920	Hawick War Memorial
1926	Henry Scott Riddell Monument on Dryden Knowes repaired
1928	Tom Scott Memorial at Selkirk
1931	Large inscribed boulder at the site of the source of the River Teviot
1934	A tablet on the wall of 37 High Street in memory of Bailie John Hardie who in 1771 brought the first stocking frames to Hawick.
1937	Cleaning and repair of Hornshole Memorial (erected in 1901).

1939	Plaque erected to mark the site of the Mercat Cross.
	Plaque erected to mark the site of the Cobble Entry.
	Plaque erected to mark the site of the Auld Brig.
1964	Tablets marking approximate sites of town's ancient ports.
1971	The Memorial Plaque in Denholm to the late Sir James A.H. Murray. The plaque was unveiled on 3 July by the Vice President. In co-operation with the Archaeological Society and the Town Council a memorial plaque to Baillie John Hardie was placed in the new Henderson Technical College to mark both the opening of the College and the bi-centenary of the knitwear trade in Hawick.
1980	Plaque erected at the birthplace of Frances George Scott to commemorate the centenary of his birth.
1990	Plaque erected in Wellogate Cemetery commemorating Ex Cornet J.E.D. Murray.
1994	Plaques marking the position of the four former tolls of the town.
1998	The Club was instrumental in having the Adam Robson painting "Homage to Tom Scott" purchased by the Hawick Common Good Fund for display in Drumlanrig's Tower.

Centenary Dinner, 2004

Earl of Dalkeith signing attendance book.

Photo: Val Watts

Photo: Val Watts

*Top Table Guests Centenary Dinner
27th February 2004*

*Front row: Earl of Dalkeith,
President Thomas M Hartop,
Hon. Provost Zandra Elliot,
Hon Secretary R W Laidlaw,
Rev E P Lindsay Thomson,
Vice President Ex.Cornet C McCrerie
A P Penman, Cornet G Mcleod, M C Aitken
Hon. Treasurer R S Elliot,
K Wilson, I M Landles*

Centenary Committee

Front row: J Coltman, President T M Hurtop, Hon Secretary R W Laidlaw,
Vice President C McCrerie
A J Neilson, S Barker, Ex.Cornet C Imrie
Hon.Treasurer R S Elliot, I M Landles, M Richardson, Ex.Cornet A P Murray
A P Penman, B King, A Pow
W T Scott, T Holmes, Past President R Muir, R Telfer, Past President D R H Nuttall

Photo: Val Watts